How to Start a Trucking Company

Avoid Common Mistakes and Learn What It Takes to See Success in This Industry

Colton Ryder

© **Copyright 2019 - All rights reserved.**

The content contained within this book may not be reproduced, duplicated or transmitted without direct written permission from the author or the publisher.

Under no circumstances will any blame or legal responsibility be held against the publisher, or author, for any damages, reparation, or monetary loss due to the information contained within this book. Either directly or indirectly.

Legal Notice:

This book is copyright protected. This book is only for personal use. You cannot amend, distribute, sell, use, quote or paraphrase any part, or the content within this book, without the consent of the author or publisher.

Disclaimer Notice:

Please note the information contained within this document is for educational and entertainment purposes only. All effort has been executed to present accurate, up to date, and reliable, complete information. No warranties of any kind are declared or implied. Readers acknowledge that the author is not engaging in the rendering of legal, financial, medical or professional advice. The content within this book has been derived from various sources. Please consult a licensed professional before attempting any techniques outlined in this book. By reading this document, the reader agrees that under no circumstances is the author responsible for any losses, direct or indirect, which are incurred as a result of the use of information contained within this document, including, but not limited to—errors, omissions, or inaccuracies.

Table of Contents

Chapter 1: Benefits of Starting a Trucking Company..6
Chapter 2: Setting Up Your Business Plan...............15
Chapter 3: Choosing Your Business Entity.............27
Chapter 4: What to Consider Before Getting Started...43
Chapter 5: How to Hire Winning Employees that Will Exponentially Grow Your Business.................83
Chapter 6: The Best Way to Get Freight for Your Business...112
Chapter 7: Common Mistakes that Could Run You Out of Business..124
Chapter 8: The Proper Trucking Business Mindset You Must Have in Order to Succeed......................133

Introduction

Trucking is one of the most lucrative businesses for startups because it's possible to start the business with one truck. The trucking industry offers very important services of transportation to various industries; hence it has a long lifespan.

In America, trucking is one of the fastest growing industries based on the high number of trucking companies being registered and the great number of people employed at trucking companies. Quite a few trucking companies are also small-scale and this should encourage you to start your own business.

The large carriers can be intimidating but remember that most of them also started from where you stand right now. All that is required for you to succeed in the trucking industry is a positive attitude, great organization, and continuous learning about the industry because things can change every day.

This book will provide you with all you need to know about the trucking business and how to go about starting your own trucking company. It aims to equip you with not only the expected but also the unexpected things that you're likely to encounter.

It will guide you through every necessary step and give you the courage and confidence you need to succeed in your trucking business. It will point out some of the things that are overlooked by many startups; like a professional e-business card, a unique logo that helps you to stand out, using social media to create awareness about your business, and maintaining good cash flow.

Finally, getting feedback, which will play a major role in helping you figure out what you're doing right and what you're doing wrong. Customer feedback will allow you to make the necessary changes to improve your operations.

Chapter 1: Benefits of Starting a Trucking Company

This chapter will begin by taking you through the logistics of the trucking industry. It will also answer questions that may be weighing on your mind. You'll have a clear picture of how the trucking business makes money.

The various underlying factors that you need to put into consideration when starting your trucking business will be clearly outlined.

The main goal of starting any business is to make money that turns into profits. There are other benefits to starting a business that you'll get to enjoy.

Before we talk about the benefits of starting a trucking company, it's paramount that you understand the importance of logistics to your trucking company.

Trucking logistics involves the management of operations to ensure all activities of the business run smoothly. This includes planning accordingly, the organization of goods, and having the proper documentation, among many others. Proper logistics management ensures efficient and timely services to customers.

Customers choose trucking companies based on the quality of service, which gives them the confidence to trust another company with their goods. Proper logistics management combined with exceptional truck drivers and reliable equipment offers adequate supply to the available demand.

Areas of business logistics that benefit the trucking business

1. **Warehousing** - This is the core area of trucking companies. It holds a great amount of the company's assets and production. A warehouse benefits your trucking business in terms of providing space for the storage of goods before they're dispatched. Lack of storage space will render your trucking business ineffective, therefore it should be a top priority. Logistic solutions showing goods for delivery and for disposal should be accurately and clearly assigned.

2. **Efficient back office** – This is where planning, communication, and documentation are managed. An office helps in ensuring that your schedules are well planned so that you're able to tell what deliveries are to be made and what needs to be dispatched. This in turn aids in giving the customers accurate information about the exact date and time they can pick up their freight.

Logistics perspective on business

The two types of transportation logistics that are used in the trucking businesses are as follows:

Outbound logistics – Goods that are distributed from a company to their customer.

Inbound logistics – Goods that are received from a third-party source, such as raw materials for production or stock.

In both outbound and inbound logistics, the main

requirements include the scheduled Estimated Time of Arrival (ETA) and official documents such as Delivery Receipts (DR), Invoices, Bill of Landing (BOL) and Certificate of Compliance.

Warehousing is an essential part of logistics management. For goods to be stored properly, there must be adequate space available at specific times. To ensure space, it's essential for a purchase order (PO) to include delivery schedules to avoid going over capacity.

Data management is important in the trucking business. Data software stores client information, manages delivery schedules, determines truck maintenance times, locates cargo, and organizes other complicated operational services of a trucking business.

Importance of logistics solutions for trucking companies

1- **Meeting customers' needs** - In order to meet customers' needs, trucking companies are required to operate with flexibility and swiftness. Owning a transportation logistics software will equip your trucking business with the ability to deliver an efficient operation of service to the stakeholders. It will also help your trucking business to act in accordance with the greater standard requirement for a professional trucking company.

2- **Easing the distribution process** - The storage of cargo and the safe delivery to various destinations are monitored by the personnel, which in turn brings down costs in the distribution process.

3- **Maintaining schedules** - Delivery schedules are processed smoothly, therefore striking a balance between the available trucks and truck drivers. By doing so, timely and safe delivery of goods by trucking companies improves their services and profitability over time.

4- **Smooth operations** - Employing logistic solutions provides an organized smooth-running process of your human resources, routine plans, fleet availability, maintenance, and data management needed to keep your operation agile, straightforward and methodical.

5- **Reduces cost of manpower** - The trucking business is highly operational without the use of a lot of manpower. Affordable technology is available to keep track of day-to-day business operations.

6- **Order fulfillment** – Logistics enables delivery of goods as per customers' detailed specifications thereby ensuring that customer requests are fulfilled.

Outsourcing and third-party (3PL) logistics

Outsourcing in the trucking business is a way of distributing work for a cheaper cost. Outsourcing and third-party logistics involve the services of other companies to act in accordance with the requirement of a client.

It comes in the form of third-party warehousing or by leasing space from another warehouse. The most popular way of outsourcing in this industry is by using additional trucks that may be required for the delivery of goods or equipment.

It's important to note that most companies outsource their trucking needs when special trucks are required for one time or occasional delivery of certain goods. For instance, a textile manufacturing company that operates regular delivery trucks may need to relocate or sell one of their machines that needs a trailer to transport the equipment.

Licensing, importation, and exportation

As part of logistics, licensing will play an integral part in order to ensure that you act in accordance with the legal requirements of each commodity. Whether your trucking business falls under importation or exportation, trucking services should have the right documents to be able to manage their services. You will be responsible for licensing since it depends on the company or the shipper but never on a third-party trucking company.

Logistics computerization

In the trucking industry, the computerization of dispatching time and route has made things easier. This has been made possible by using the GPRS, which has enabled companies to track down their trucks and their current status.

It has also added security to truck drivers, the company, and the goods as well. This GPRS automation has rendered an easier task in the trucking world as it provides a wireless solution for monitoring the handling and transportation of goods as well as managing the delivery schedules and trucking services based on the clients' needs.

The availability of this kind of safety innovation has also attracted insurance companies to take part in the business of trucking. As one of the most in-demand businesses, trucking companies capitalize on the growing improvement of modernization and automation. With the aid of modern transportation logistics solutions, they're able to minimize costs while improving the efficiency of their trucking services.

Therefore, now is the best time for you to start your trucking business.

How to make money in the Trucking business

By now the important question on your mind is, how do I make money in this business? Simply put, you make money by transporting goods for your customers either directly or through freight brokers. For your business to realize profits, several factors have to be considered.

1. Finding the right market niche

You should consider the right market niche by going after the markets avoided by large carriers. This means focusing on hauling goods such as food grade liquids, livestock, fresh produce, and meat. Taking fresh produce and meat as an example, one reduces competition, maintains work throughout the year, and counteracts recessions.

You'll be guaranteed consistency since fresh produce and meat are regularly transported all over the country. Access to local produce markets, farms, or directly from wholesalers provides stability and good profitability.

2. Charging the right rate

You should consider having the right rates in order to make profits. This involves finding out how much the brokers pay, getting to a load board, getting more loads headed towards the same direction, knowing how much the shippers are paid by the brokers and knowing the rates for specific lanes. As you do all these, keep in mind that your rates should bring you good profits while at the same time cover all your operating costs.

3. Establish your operation costs

For you to make a profit, it's important to know your costs of operation. This is achieved by determining the fixed costs and the variable costs. Fixed costs are the costs that remain constant in your business whether your trucks are on the road or parked. Examples include permits, insurance, truck payments etc. Variable costs are derived from the number of miles driven by the trucks which obviously vary depending on the distance covered.

4. Minimal use of brokers and load boards

Working directly with your customer enables the establishment of a reliable relationship. This can be made possible by offering your customer more competitive rates than those offered by brokers, while at the same time eliminating a percentage of the money that goes to the brokers. In this case, you get to keep the whole amount.

5. Running an efficient office

For a startup, you can work from home if you have a computer, a printer, and access to the internet. You'll also need an accounting software and you're good to go. As your business grows you'll grow with it and get a space to rent.

Benefits of starting a trucking business

The following are the benefits of starting a trucking business.

1. Independence

By starting a trucking business, you get to make your own decisions from what to haul, when to work and who to work with. You'll also have total control of your income, which could lead to financial freedom.

2. Flexibility

The trucking business offers flexibility by enabling you to make your own schedule allowing you to work when it's convenient for you. This is made possible whether you're an owner-operator or employ truck drivers. You can broker or deal directly with shippers and you don't have to be tied to one customer.

3. Profitability

Starting a trucking business enables you to be in control of the rates you charge. If you're an owner-operator, you keep the profit accrued from the business. Once you build relationships and maintain great customer service, you will be able to enjoy the generated revenue which in turn leads to profits.

4. Variety of customers

Transportation is key to various industries; from farmers, to manufacturers, to merchants, and contractors. These industries create several market niches to choose from; including food deliveries, courier firms, private carriers and carriers for hire.

This business stands out compared to other businesses which are mostly limited to a specific industry in which to operate.

5. Availability of opportunities

Despite trucking being one of the most competitive businesses in existence, there is still room for start-ups who mostly start as owner–operators or carriers for hire. The trucking business also experiences a shortage of truck drivers hence it offers opportunities for new drivers who have obtained a CDL (Commercial Driver's License). This is not the case in other businesses where you find unhealthy competition due to market saturation.

Chapter 2: Setting up Your Business Plan

Now that you know how to start your trucking business, this chapter will give you knowledge on drawing a business plan and the essentials of it which include creating a mission and vision statement, conducting competitor analysis, and calculating the cost of starting a trucking company among other things.

A trucking company, just like any other business, requires a business plan, which is the mirror of the business. It's a clear reflection of the business, which is not only useful for personal purpose, but it's vital for seeking prospective partners, investors or financial assistance from banks.

Your business plan should contain a clear mapped out plan on what the company does, what it stands for, what sets it apart from its competitors, future predictions of the company's financial position, and how you plan to achieve the goals that you have set out for yourself.

Remember that a business plan is a continuous process that requires you to review and update it regularly to ensure that you meet your goals. It's also important to note that every business plan is unique and to this effect, yours should stand out.

The following outlines the key elements in a trucking company business plan:

1. Executive summary

This is an introduction of your company and what it hopes to achieve in the future. It should cover a maximum of two pages and a minimum of one page. It should be clear, concise, and interesting to the reader. It should outline the company's objectives and how they will be met. This should also feature the company's mission, its services, financial information, its performance, and intended future plans. This is also known as the company's profile.

2. Company description

This part gives an overall description of your company's vision and mission and why its unique compared to its competitors. It should have information on the founder, why it was started, the year it was started, the business location, and the specific goods you intend to haul. As your company grows, this is where you will include the organization structure. It's important to know that a vision statement is different from a mission statement.

Mission statement

A mission statement clearly outlines what your company does, why it does it and the benefits of what it does. It shows what your company aims to achieve and the path it will take in the future. It makes your company stand out from its competitors and it outlines the common goal that your company and future employees need to achieve. It should be an eloquent and memorable sentence.

Creating a mission statement

a) Define your purpose

This should answer questions like why does your company exist? Who does it aim to serve? How will you deliver the service and why is your service valuable? Think of the benefits in terms of impact on the community, employees, shareholders, or customers.

b) Be particular

This simply means avoid any jargons. It should be easy to remember in order for it to communicate well with the intended members, for example employees. Choose your words carefully and ensure that the terms are understandable and relevant to your business.

c) Inspire

Make it dynamic and inspirational to encourage your employees to work hard towards the company's vision.

d) Be brief

While large companies have a lengthy mission statement, making it short and concise is the most ideal way of remembering your company's core values, which will guide you in the years to come.

Vision statement

A vision statement paints a picture of the desired future. It's a description of what the future will be like if the business manages to fulfill its mission. It involves your imagination and dreaming big about your company. It's meant to inspire your employees to achieve the company's goals.

Your company's brand values should be reflected in your vision statement. Your vision statement should be a reflection of how you want your employees to act and behave. Stop and think about what it is that you really want your company to achieve and don't hold anything back.

Creating a vision statement

a) Examine your mission statement

This simply involves writing down what your company does and what purpose it serves. Your mission statement should be able to answer that. Put it into the present tense.

b) Make it memorable

Dare to dream in order to make it powerful. Ensure that it's to the point and easy to remember. It should answer the questions, what is unique about your services? What will your company be remembered for?

c) Shaping your vision formula

Apply this formula:

Five years from now, (my company name) will..........................by...........................

This formula will help you to identify the accomplishment that you consider to be most important and how to accomplish it within a certain timeline. For instance:

Five years from now, (my company name) will be the top-grossing trucking service provider in South Coast area by consistently providing reliable and affordable services to farmers.

d) Be committed to the vision

Exert your vision statement in your business planning since it provides your destination. It will help you achieve all of your goals. Ensure you constantly share it with employees and potential partners by printing it out and sticking it where it will be visible and act as a reminder.

Major differences between mission statements and vision statements are:

a) A mission statement talks about how the business will get to where it wants to be, whereas a vision statement talks about where the business wants to be.

b) A mission statement gives answers to the questions "what do we do? What makes us unique?" While a vision statement answers the question "where do we aim to be?"

c) A mission statement is based on the present while a vision statement is based on the future.

d) A mission statement addresses both the internal and external members whereas a vision statement addresses the internal members only.

3. Services

Clearly outline the goods that your trucking company will haul and the industries that you will work with. Show that your services are important as they meet the needs demanded by the customer. An example could be something such as transporting fresh produce for farmers to a part of the country where many carriers do not venture.

4. Market Analysis

This section should demonstrate how conversant you are with your trucking business in terms of customer needs, what is trending, and why you believe your company can thrive in the already crowded trucking market. The following key points should form the basis of your market analysis:

a) Trucking industry description

You should have great knowledge of the size of the trucking industry by being able to identify the major carriers and the biggest shippers.

b) Target market

You should show that your trucking company stands out by specializing in a market that is avoided by large carriers, hence guaranteeing you great returns.

c) Unique characteristics

Identify customer needs that stand out and how your trucking company intends to meet those needs.

d) Size of main target market

Have concrete knowledge on your high-ranking market as well as the top customers. For instance, if your area is dominated by cattle farmers, there is a need for transporting the cattle to the slaughterhouse. Knowing the actual number of cattle farmers who are your target market is critical.

e) Market share

This should show how much market your company intends to penetrate within a specific period. The prediction must be reasonable.

f) Pricing and gross margin targets

Clearly outline your trucking company's charging rates and any discounts that may be given. Include your target margin for each service you offer.

g) Competitive analysis

This shows that you have done your due diligence on your competitors. You must know their strengths and weaknesses. Conducting a SWOT analysis is highly recommended.

SWOT analysis

It's an acronym that stands for Strengths, Weaknesses, Opportunities, and Threats. Strengths and weaknesses are internal factors that are subject to change if you work on them, for example reputation and sales. Opportunities and Threats on the other hand, are external factors that you have no control over, for example prices and competitors.

Strengths – Identify what your trucking company is good at and what makes it stand out from its competitors, for instance having a strong brand or unique technology. It's advisable to take into consideration both the internal view of your strengths and the external view from customers and those in the same market.

Weaknesses – Identify the things that hinder your best performance. These are the areas of your trucking business that require improvement, for example poor customer service or poor location. Be realistic and consider both the internal and external perspectives.

Opportunities – This refers to the external factors that favor your trucking business. A keen look at your strengths and weaknesses could help point out any untapped opportunities which could be brought out by things such as changes in government regulations in your field or changes in technology.

Threats – This refers to anything that could potentially harm your trucking business. This includes existing or potential competitors, changes in customer preferences, or new government regulations that could reduce your sales.

Conducting a SWOT analysis will enable your business to compete strategically within the market.

a) Regulations

You should have knowledge of government regulations that can affect your trucking business. For example, changes in fuel prices or food safety rules.

5. Sales and Marketing

Strategizing how to gain the market share involves:

a) Marketing strategy

Take into consideration how you will promote and market your trucking business. You have the option of hiring an external firm or you could do the marketing on your own, for instance having fliers printed and distributing them. Ensure that you have the costs that you will spend on marketing and advertising and identify the media through which you will communicate. Some of these include local business magazines, posters, social media etc. As you include all these, keep in mind your target regions and industries that you're trying to reach.

b) Sales strategy

This is where you lay out plans on how you intend to sell your trucking services to potential customers with a view of generating revenue and in turn maximizing your profits. It involves identifying your target market and how you will appeal to them. You can employ the use of external sales agents or hire salespeople for your trucking company.

6. Financial projections

This section clearly outlines your trucking company's financial position based on capital which is the startup cost and the anticipated regular monthly expenses of running your business. There could never be an exact cost for starting a trucking business as the prices could vary based on your location, goods you haul, and business size. Using America as an example, the following should guide you as you carry out your personal research, just to ensure that you don't leave anything out.

a) Buying the trucks

First, you need to determine the trucks you want to buy and the price at which you will get them. It's wise for a start-up company to go for a second-hand truck cab which could cost as little as 20,000 or so, as opposed to spending around

$113,000 to upwards of $180,000 on a new truck cab. This of course isn't even considering the cost of the trailer, which can cost another $30,000-$75,000 depending on what you get. If this option proves to be difficult for you, there is still an option of seeking companies that can allow you to pay in installments.

b) Registration

Once you have bought your truck, you need to have it registered with the department of motor vehicles or any other regulatory agencies in your area of operation. You will spend at least $500 to be able to get this done.

c) Business Licenses and Permits

You will need to get a business license and permits that will allow you to run your trucking business, drive past your border and carry specific goods with specific weights. It is difficult trying to find the right website that will help in obtaining permits. There are websites that list all of the requirements needed according to your particular state of operation. These sites will also guide you on the DOT requirements as well as how to obtain a CDL.

d) Insurance

This business requires that you carry insurance. Transporting valuable goods carries the risk of damage, loss or other unforeseen risks. You must also insure all drivers who will be on the road.

Insurance in the business of trucking is not a one-off expense rather it will be a regular expense. Allocate an annual budget of $1,000 to $2,000 if you are the owner-operator on lease and $8,000 to $12,000 plus if you are the owner-operator under your own authority.

e) Office / Parking space

As a start-up, you could operate from your home or rent office space. Include this cost if it's the latter. You must, however, get a secure parking space for your truck which will cost you some money. This will be a regular monthly expense.

f) Website and load board

It's important to set up a website as you start your business. You could do it yourself with the help of online programs or seek the services of a website developer. Either way, you'll most likely incur a cost of between $100 and $200 to get this done. Setting up the load board and accessing customers will also incur an extra cost which you must include in your calculations.

g) Marketing and promotion

Include the cost of marketing and promoting your trucking business which you have to research for estimates. Get quotes for the cost of creating the company logo, branding your truck with the name of your company and logo, creating and printing brochures, business cards, and other materials for promoting your company. Depending on the area you want to reach, estimate at least $500 for all of these expenses. Marketing and promotion will fall under regular monthly expenses as well.

h) Staffing

As you start, you can be the driver, accountant, and receptionist at the same time, but as your company grows, there will be so much to do which you will eventually find overwhelming. You will have to share and delegate various tasks to ensure your business runs smoothly. Put into consideration the cost of hiring staff and paying salaries, wages, insurance, etc. which will all be regular expenses.

i) Maintenance costs

This is an unforeseen cost that can happen anytime the truck breaks down or requires routine maintenance. Make sure that you budget for this expense in your regular monthly expenses.

j) Miscellaneous

This is extra money that may come in handy in case of a business emergency or any other need that may arise.

Therefore, the total cost of starting a trucking business is at least $ 10,000 for a single truck and $50,000 plus for having a number of trucks.

Chapter 3: Choosing your Business Entity

In this chapter, you will learn about the various business entities and how they work. It's important to decide the business structure that best fits your trucking company. You will also learn about opening a business bank account as well as obtaining an Employer Identification Number.

Part of starting your trucking business requires you to choose the business entity that it will be. It's the structure you will adopt in running your business.

It's paramount to have knowledge of the types of business entities that exist because they will ensure that you operate within the legal structures. The entities act as a guide on how your business will operate internally.

They also vary in terms of taxation and liabilities and as such they all have their advantages and disadvantages. There are six types of business entities and they are as follows:

a) Sole Proprietorship

A sole proprietorship, just like the name suggests is a business owned and operated by one person. It's the simplest form of a business entity as it does not require registration apart from licenses and permits in your industry. If you start your trucking business alone, you automatically become a sole proprietor under the law.

Pros

a) Easy to start – It's easy to start as there is no need for registration.

b) Fast decision making - Decision making is fast since there is no need for consultation.

c) No double taxation - There is no double taxation since the business and the owner are treated as one hence business income is reported on a personal income tax return.

d) Taxes are paid on income generated from the business only.

e) In case the business makes a profit, the owner gets to enjoy all of it since he/she is the sole proprietor.

Cons

a) Unlimited liability - this means that in case the business is unable to offset its debts and liabilities, the owner's personal assets such as your cars or home can be taken to offset them.

b) Tax charges on your Social Security/Medicare are double the amount you would pay as an employee.

c) If the business runs into losses, the owner bears the burden alone.

d) Securing a business loan from lenders is difficult since there is no separation between you and the business.

e) Most startups are sole proprietorships because of the simplicity involved in setting it up. Unfortunately, with no separation between the owner and the business, there is an unlimited liability which can be very risky. As a result, most of these businesses revert to LLCs or Corporations.

b) General Partnerships

A general partnership, unlike a sole proprietorship is owned and operated by two or more people who are partners. They all contribute towards raising the capital for starting the business and take part in making decisions together. Below are the pros and cons of entering into a general partnership.

Pros

a) Easy to start – it's easy to start since it doesn't require registration.

b) In case the business incurs losses, it's divided by the partners and the burden is shared.

c) Less capital required– all the partners contribute towards raising the capital versus trying to raise it on your own.

d) Consultation – there must be consultation among the partners in case a decision needs to be made, thereby ensuring they make the best decision.

e) The business losses can be deducted from the partner's personal tax returns.

f) No double taxation – the business and owners are viewed as one hence the business income is reported on each partner's personal income tax return.

Cons

a) Unlimited liability – the partners remain liable for the

business debts and liabilities. If the business is unable to repay its debts, the partners' personal assets can be used to settle the debts.

b) Disputes arising among the partners could affect the business negatively.

c) In some states, the partners are personally liable for each other's careless behavior.

d) Obtaining loans for a business that lacks registration is difficult.

e) Partnerships are mostly formed by startups to lower the risks that come with starting a business on your own. They offer a great support system, but you should be very careful with the people you choose to enter into partnerships with.

c) Limited Partnership

Limited partnership business entities must be formed by registration which entails filing paperwork with the state. There are two types of partners in a Limited Partnership;

General partners - those who own, manage the operations, and bear the liabilities of the business.

Limited partners – those who act as investors and are not involved in the business operations. Their liability is limited to their capital contribution hence they are also referred to as silent partners.

The following are the pros and cons of a Limited Partnership:

Pros

1. The general partners can acquire the money they need for the business while they carry on with operations.

2. A limited partnership offers an alternative option for raising money from investors who have no personal liability.

3. In the event that a limited partner wants to leave it does not require the partnership to be dissolved.

Cons

1. Limited partners risk having personal liability if they unintentionally get too involved in the business operations.

2. It's more expensive to create a Limited partnership than a general partnership.

3. General partners are held liable for the company's debts and liabilities.

Business owners with multiple businesses thrive in Limited Partnerships since they can bring in investors who have limited liability.

d) *Limited Liability Company (LLC)*

A Limited Liability Company (LLC) is a form of business with one or more members. Starting an LLC requires filing the Articles of Association with the Secretary of State. There are two types of partners in an LLC; partners who own the LLC and are viewed as the investors who have limited liability and partners who manage the operations of the LLC and have unlimited liability. The relationships and operations are guided by an LLC Agreement. Below are the pros and cons of an LLC.

Pros

1. Limited liability – the owners are not personally liable for the business debts or liabilities.

2. Flexibility - The members get to instruct the IRS how to tax their LLC either as a partnership or as a Corporation.

3. Forming an LLC does not take long since it only requires registration with the Secretary of State.

4. The members are not personally responsible for each other's careless behavior.

5. There is no double taxation since its charged on either the personal level or the corporate level, but not both.

Cons

1. It's more expensive to set up an LLC than a sole proprietorship or general partnership.

2. Partners in charge of operations are liable for any debt incurred by the business since they have unlimited liability.

3. The business is likely to be affected by any disagreements among partners.

Limited Liability Companies are mostly preferred by small businesses because it integrates sole proprietorship or partnerships with the legal protection of corporations.

e) C – Corporation

C – Corporation is a type of business entity where the owners are the shareholders. Forming a corporation involves many regulations and tax laws that must be adhered to. The shareholders elect a board of directors who are responsible for managing and operating the business. The directors have the power to hire and fire employees, as well as make decisions that are in the best interest of the business and are in line with the business objectives. The employees also have the responsibility of ensuring that they work towards realizing the business goals that have been set within the specified period.

A corporation is a separate legal entity from its owners, meaning the owners have limited liability. A corporation can buy property, sue and get sued. It can also sell stock in the stock exchange market for the purpose of raising capital. It can change ownership and continue to exist.

The operations of a corporation are guided by corporation by-laws which are subject to revision as the corporation grows. Annual shareholder meetings are held to give updates on the performance of the corporation.

Below are the pros and cons of a Corporation:

Pros

   a) The owners, who are the shareholders are not liable for the debts and liabilities of the corporation.

   b) Corporations are entitled to more tax deductions compared to other types of business entities.

   c) Since corporations can sell stock in the stock market,

they have the capacity to raise more capital.

d) The ownership of a corporation is easily transferable, which means that in the event that the owners foresee the business sinking, they can sell it without having to lose their capital investment.

e) The employees enjoy the benefits of not getting taxed health insurance premiums and life insurance which are fully deductible as corporate expenses.

Cons

- Forming a corporation is more expensive than other business entities.

- There is double taxation since the corporation is taxed as well as the shareholder's income, which is levied on the dividends.

- A lot of paperwork is involved when starting a corporation including legal paperwork that must be filed with the Secretary of State.

- The shareholders have no control over the operation of the corporation.

- Decision making involves a long process since the directors must be consulted.

- Business losses can't be deducted on the owners' personal tax return.

- There are many corporate formalities, such as shareholders meetings and by-laws.

Most startups do not opt to start a corporation because of the complexities involved but as your business grows, it offers more legal protections.

f) S Corporations

The taxation process is the only feature that distinguishes a c corp from an s corp. While in a c corp there is double taxation including corporate tax and shareholders personal income tax, the s corp has pass-through taxation, which means that the profits and losses are passed through to the owners' personal tax return. S corps are required to file their taxes annually whereas c corps file their taxes quarterly.

Below are the pros and cons before you consider adding an 's' to your corp.

Pros

1) The shareholders who are the owners do not have personal liability on business debts and liabilities.
2) Double taxation is eliminated since only the owner's income is taxed on their personal tax return.
3) Availability of investment opportunities through the sale of stock in the stock market.
4) Owners report profits and losses in their personal tax return since it's pass-through taxation.
5) It has immortal existence. The business continues to exist even if the owner dies or leaves it.

Cons

1) It's expensive to form and still incurs ongoing

> expenses such as franchise tax fees.
>
> 2) Unlike the rest of the business entities, you must be a legal resident of the U.S.
>
> 3) Ownership is limited since there can't be more than 100 shareholders.
>
> 4) Several corporate formalities are involved, such as annual shareholders meetings.

Converting your business to an s corp requires filing an IRS Form 2553. It can be good for a business that requires a corporate structure with tax flexibility like that of a sole proprietorship.

Determining the best entity for your trucking business

By now you have some fundamental knowledge of how to start your trucking business and the necessary steps involved. At this point, it's important that you choose the right business entity for your startup business. It's advisable to seek consultation from a business lawyer and a tax professional on the business entity that matches your needs if you can afford it.

As a startup, there are three important factors to consider when choosing your business entity: -

1. Legal protection

As discussed above, sole proprietorships and partnerships have no limited liability which means you're at great legal risk. Corporations and LLCs, on the other hand, offer legal protection. It's therefore safe to say that if your business involves little legal risk, sole proprietorships and partnerships are the way to go. However, in the case of the trucking business, you will likely want to form an LLC or Corporation to help give you legal protection.

2. Taxes

Sole proprietorships and general partnerships offer the simplest taxation since it's based on a personal level.

3. Paperwork

Sole Proprietorships and General Partnerships do not require a lot of paperwork unlike corporations and LLC's.

It's possible to change your business entity at any point but it's important to note that some changes are easier to make than others. For example, converting from a Sole Proprietorship and Partnership into an LLC is as simple as filing the right paperwork. Converting to a Corporation is more difficult, especially when it comes to the issuing of stocks. Converting from a C Corporation to an S Corporation attracts unprecedented taxes.

The IRS also has restrictions and deadlines imposed on how many times you can change your type of business entity. All business types are different, and all businesses have different needs. Consider the pros and cons of each entity and ensure you consult a business lawyer and a tax profession for guidance on which path to undertake.

Obtaining an Employer Identification Number

Having gone through the above documents required for the various business entities, you may have realized that you need an Employer Identification Number (EIN). An Employer Identification Number is a unique nine-digit number issued to businesses by the Internal Revenue Service (IRS) for taxation purposes.

There are three ways of applying for an Employer Identification Number (EIN)

1. **Apply online** - The fastest and easiest way of obtaining an Employer Identification Number (EIN) is by applying for it online on the Internal Revenue Service (IRS) website. Once your information is processed and validated, you're immediately issued with your Employer Identification Number (EIN). For online applications, you're required to have your trucking business based in the U.S and you must have a valid Taxpayer Identification Number. Make sure you print out the confirmation after completing the application.

2. **Apply by fax** - You can also apply for your Employer Identification Number through fax by downloading the Form SS-4 from the Internal Revenue Service (IRS) website, filling it in and sending it via fax. It takes roughly four days to receive it via fax.

3. **Apply by mail** - You can also apply by mail which involves filling the Form SS-4 and mailing it to the IRS in your state. It will take around four weeks to receive it by mail in most cases.

It's also important to note that the calendar begins on the date you obtain the Employer Identification Number (EIN).

The IRS created a PDF pamphlet for every business structure that guides you on how to fill out your form.

Getting a Business Bank Account

Opening a bank account for your business is key. It helps you to separate your business finances from your personal finances. Before knowing how to go about opening a business account, let's look at the importance of separating it from your personal account:

1. Clean and accurate bookkeeping

Separating your trucking business transactions from your personal transactions prevents a mix up between the two. It helps to ensure that you obtain clean records for the purposes of accounting. Your bank statements should match your receipts and invoices when it's time to file your income tax returns.

2. Demonstrates the seriousness of your business

When you separate the trucking business account from your personal account it helps to show how seriously you take the business.

3. It's a Requirement for incorporated businesses

If your company is a separate legal entity (such as a corporation or LLC), then the IRS requires that you have a separate business account from your personal account.

4. Auditing

Separating your business account from your personal account ensures that you keep clean records and a paper trail which is necessary if the IRS decides to conduct an audit on your trucking business.

5. Professionalism

Having a separate business account enhances professionalism. Whenever you write a check, it identifies with your trucking company which enhances your professional image.

6. Financial position

Having a separate trucking business account from your personal account helps you to know the amount of money your business has which also aids in creating budgets and cash flows projections.

Steps in Opening a Business Bank Account

1. Choose a bank

The first step requires you to decide on a bank. This involves identifying the needs of your trucking business. Consider your current needs and what you may need in the future. Ask yourself if you need a bank that offers incentives or features such as cash management, deposit reconciliation, or mobile check depositing services.

Inquire about required account minimum balances and opening fees if there are any. Decide if you need the money in your account to earn interest.

Consider opening your trucking business account at the same bank where you have your personal account, as it will ease the burden of having to move from one bank to another. You might also receive additional perks since you're already an account holder.

2. Prepare documents

The next step involves getting your business paperwork together depending on your business structure. All businesses must have a Taxpayer Identification Number which is either going to be your Social Security Number or Employer Identification Number depending on what your business entity is. If your business is a partnership, corporation or if you have employees, then applying for an Employer Identification Number is a requirement. It's important to note that a Social Security Number is a Tax Identification Number of an individual, while Employer Identification Number (EIN) is a tax identification number of a business. The following are the required documents needed for each business entity:

1. **Sole Proprietorship**

- Security Social Number or Employer Identification Number
- Business license or business name filing document

2. **Partnerships**

- Employer Identification Number
- Business name filing document
- Partnership Agreement

3. **Corporations**
- Employer Identification Number
- Articles of Incorporation

4. **Limited Liability Company (LLCs)**
- Security Social Number or Employer Identification Number
- Articles of Organization

3. **Open the account online or in person**

After choosing a bank and gathering the required documents, you're now able to open an account which can be done online or by going to the bank in person. It's important to note that some businesses such as telemarketing, precious stones, or gambling require you to go to the bank in person. However, since you're starting a trucking business that shouldn't be a problem.

Consider opening an account online if you want to complete the process by yourself, but if you want to ask questions and get clarifications, you should go to the bank in person. It's advisable for you to go in person to open your account. The reason for this is that it gives you a greater advantage of being assisted on the available account features. It also gives you the chance to get some financial advice as well as any clarifications on things that you might not be sure of.

4. **Verification**

Now that you've set up your trucking business account, confirm that every detail is correct and that everything runs smoothly in your day-to-day transactions.

Chapter 4: What to Consider Before Getting Started

This chapter will dive deeper into important things that you need to consider before starting your trucking company. Expect to learn about insurance, fuel card services, management software, required licenses, etc.

Having knowledge on all of these different things will ensure that you don't leave room for a trial and error situation in your business.

There are many factors that you should put into consideration before you embark on your trucking business.

Getting the right kind and amount of insurance

Insurance is a prerequisite in starting a trucking business and it's the largest expense you'll need to budget for. The trucking business falls under semi-truck insurance, which is also known as owner-operator truck insurance. The coverage you need and the related costs of covering your truck will depend on the status of your owner-operator, which varies widely. The two status are:

Leased owner-operator – This means that you're under lease to a motor carrier. The cost of the coverage will be lower since the carrier covers part of the insurance. This cover costs between $1,500 and $2,000 annually.

Owner-operator with authority – this means that the

owner-operator working under his/her own authority bears all the insurance costs and related costs of covering the truck. This makes the coverage more expensive and could cost between $8,000 and $12,500 plus.

There are six main types of owner-operator-truck insurance:

1. Public Liability Insurance

Public liability insurance covers any physical injury and damage of property suffered by third-parties. It's a requirement for owner-operators working under their own authority by the Federal Motor Carrier Safety Administration (FMCSA).

They're also required to take a proof of liability insurance before obtaining their commercial driver's license (CDL). Public liability premium cost is between $5,000 and $7,000 annually with an average coverage limit of a $750,000 to $1 million as the minimum.

It's also required for leased owner-operators, but the motor carrier incurs the cost of this insurance on their behalf.

2. General Liability Insurance

This coverage is wider than public liability as it not only covers risks associated with your truck but other risks in your day-to-day operations such as accidents in your office. It's not a law requirement, but it's needed by carriers and it's advisable for owner-operators under their own authority to take it up. General liability premium ranges from $750 to $1,200 annually with an average limit of $1 million.

3. Non-trucking Liability Insurance

This coverage is mainly for owner-operators under lease with a motor carrier. It covers damages and injuries caused to third parties while driving for personal purposes. It's not required by law, but it is usually recommended. Non-trucking liability premium cost is over $450 annually as it could vary.

4. Bobtail Insurance

Bobtail was an original description of an owner-operator truck without an attached trailer. It covers you and your owner-operator truck while doing business, but it does not include hauling a load. Owner-operators under lease need this coverage which is paid for by the motor carriers. This premium costs between $350 and $400 annually with a minimum limit of $1 million.

5. Physical Damage Coverage

This coverage will pay for all the truck's costs of damages and repairs, which include theft, natural disasters, vandalism etc. It's recommended for both owner-operators under lease and owner-operators with authority. Although it's not required by law, it's usually necessary to secure a loan. Physical damage premiums go for $2,000 to $3,000 annually or it could be based on a certain percentage of your truck's value. The average is the actual or stated value of your truck.

6. Motor Truck Cargo Coverage

Motor truck cargo coverage covers lost or damaged cargo that you're transporting. It's not a law requirement, but it is recommended for both owner-operators under lease and owner-operators with authority. The premium cost varies but the average coverage limit is $100,000.

Apart from the above main insurance coverages for owner-operator truck drivers, you may need other additional coverage on your policy for certain situations. They are as follows:

1. Trailer Interchange Insurance

Trailer interchange insurance covers physical damage. It's required when carrying a trailer full of goods belonging to someone else and the trucking company that owns the trailer doesn't have coverage for it. This coverage normally comes under either the truckers or the motor carriers' liability policy. It's recommended for both the owner-operator under authority and the owner-operator under lease. This premium ranges from $100 to $1,500 annually with the average cover limit going for $20,000 to $30,000.

2. Hazmat Truck Insurance

If you're involved in carrying hazardous materials like fuel or chemicals, you need hazmat coverage. The degree of risk related to the hazardous materials determines limits and cost of coverage. Hazmat premiums cost about $12,000 annually and have an average coverage limit of $5 million as the minimum.

3. Livestock Cargo Insurance

Just like the name suggests, livestock cargo coverage covers the risk of hauling livestock, which includes death, injury, or the animals escaping. It's not required by law but it's recommended for owner-operators who need additional liability when hauling animals. Livestock premiums go for $6,000 to $12,500 annually as the average limit varies.

4. Trucking Umbrella Insurance

This type of insurance helps to cover gaps in policies. If at any given time your main insurance coverage is too low to cover large expenses that are beyond your limit, Umbrella Insurance would cover the expense. It's not a law requirement but it's recommended for both the owner-operator under lease and the owner-operator under authority. This premium costs between $500 and $1,500 annually and has an average limit of $1 million.

5. Uninsured / Underinsured

This covers you if you're involved in an accident caused by another driver who is not insured, or their limit is not high enough to cover the damages. Although it's not a requirement by law, both the owner-operator under authority and the owner-operator under lease are strongly advised to carry it. This premium ranges from $50 to $100 with an average limit of $100,000 and $100,000 per occurrence.

6. Workers Compensation Coverage

This insurance coverage is only needed by trucking businesses that have employees. It covers injuries and disabilities sustained while on the job. It's required by law for business owners with employees. Motor carriers also need this coverage. Workers compensation premiums range from $250 to $625 with an average limit of $100,000 per occurrence and $500,000 per policy.

You should determine your own trucking company's coverage needs. Apart from the main coverage, there are other essential insurance options you'll need to add. Consulting an insurance agency will give you greater insight on which coverage to consider. You can break down annual premiums into monthly payments and limits are determined by the policy period which is normally one year.

Several factors affect the cost of semi-truck insurance hence the varying costs. They include:

- **Ownership status** – An owner-operator under lease has coverage costs reduced since the motor carrier pays for a part of the coverage whereas an owner-operator under their own authority pays for both the main and other supplemental coverage on their own, making insurance costs higher.

- **Cargo type** - The type of goods that you carry will determine the amount that the pre. Insurance companies determine charges in relation to the risk involved. Carrying hazardous goods is costlier in terms of coverage due to the high risk compared to other goods.

- **The Weight of freight** – Insurance coverage also uses the weight of the freight as a factor in determining the premium cost. The heavier the goods are, the higher the cost of coverage and vice versa.

- **Driving distance** – Insurance companies look at the distance traveled when determining the premium cost. The further the distance traveled, the more likely the risk of getting into accidents, therefore, they charge higher premiums for longer distances.

- **Truck value** – The value of the truck determines the coverage for physical damage. The higher the truck's value, the higher the premium will be.

- **Actual cash value versus the stated amount** – In the case of physical damage, the insurance companies use the actual cash value as the current market value at the time when the accident occurs.

The stated amount, on the other hand, refers to the amount stated by the driver. If your stated value is lower, then the insurance coverage will be lower. You face a great risk if your sated value is lower than the amount it would cost to replace your truck.

- **Credit history** – insurance companies will also review your credit score. If your credit score is poor, the insurance companies take it as an indication that they are at greater risk and therefore charge higher premiums.

- **Loss history** – When you have no previous claims, insurance companies offer reduced premiums.

- **CDL experience** – The more experienced you are as a driver, the lower the risk is that you carry. Carrying a Commercial Driver's License (CDL) will help lower your premium.

- **Deductible amount** – though it's not advisable, you can raise your deductible for the purpose of reducing costs if you can afford the risk. The higher the deductible the lower premium you'll pay.

- **Limits coverage** – Insurance companies base the cost of coverage on limits. The higher the limits are, the higher your premium will be.

10 Questions to Ask Before Starting a Trucking Business

1. What kind of freight do you want to haul?

Some drivers haul anything that works with their type of

trailer, while others specialize in a particular type of freight. Trailer types vary from refrigerated or flatbed, among many others. The one you use will determine the type of freight you haul. Trucks also vary and should match the needs of your operation.

2. What kind of equipment do you need?

The main equipment you'll need in a trucking business is a trailer and a truck. You should determine where you're going to operate since some trucks are best suited for long-haul operations. You should also consider equipment that is flexible in case you branch out in the future. More detailed information on equipment will be covered in one of the chapters ahead.

3. What business structure is best for you?

Do your due diligence in order to make the right choice. The various business entities have already been covered in chapter 3.

4. How will you handle repair and maintenance?

Repairs can cost your business a lot of money. The trailer may just need occasional upkeep, but the tractor undergoes the most expensive repairs. Regardless of maintenance expenses, take care of small issues before they become bigger issues. Truck stops offer shops across the nation to assist with maintenance along the way. Having a local shop you trust is the best option, but if you have mechanical experience you can perform your own maintenance and save your business a lot of money.

5. Do you have an accountant?

Whether you hire a professional tax officer, or you do your

own accounting, it's important to know about the various taxes that you're required to comply with.

They include; per diem, fuel tax, repairs and equipment, depreciation etc. Consider having a good accountant familiar with tax law, tax codes, and preferably the trucking industry because he or she will be valuable to you. This can save you a lot of headaches when it comes time to file your taxes.

6. Do you need special clearances or endorsements added to your license?

Many drivers will require a Hazardous Materials (HAZMAT) endorsement and Transportation Worker Identification Credential (TWIC) in order to transport specific freight or military installations. Special endorsements may be needed to pull certain trailer types, such as tanker, doubles, or triples.

7. What kind of business licenses and insurance do you need?

To make your company official, registering with the state is one of the major steps you must take. You can contact insurance companies that work specifically with the trucking industry. There are also insurance companies that are available for trucking companies starting a new venture.

8. Do you want to be an independent contractor or do everything yourself?

Most owner-operators start at least with a motor carrier who handles everything leaving you to just drive, maintain your truck, and prepare and pay your taxes.

Other owner-operators with their own authority handle everything themselves.

9. Do you have enough money to fund the equipment?

It's important to know that apart from other expenses when starting up, the expense of buying a truck is greater than most other expenses. Treat it like you're buying a house and be realistic by getting only what you can afford.

10. Consider joining associations

Associations like the Owner-Operator Independent Drivers Association (OOIDA) is the only group representing small business truckers to the Washington DC lawmakers. You will also get expert advice from specialists, competitive rates with lots of discounts, and convenient monthly insurance installments among other benefits. Another example is the AAOFOO American Association of Owner Operators where you get fuel discounts, accounting and bookkeeping services, equipment financing and so much more.

How to keep costs low for semi-truck insurance

Despite insurance being a major expense, especially for owner-operators under their own authority, some costs can be controlled in the following ways in order to reduce insurance costs:

1. **Package your insurance policy** – Avoid buying separate policies for your trucking business by putting them all under one policy. Doing this will reduce the cost of coverage.

2. **Maintain good driving records** – When you maintain good driving records, insurance companies consider you a low-risk customer and can therefore

lower your premium amounts.

3. **Increase deductibles and decrease limits** – The deductible and coverage limit have a direct impact on your premium. In order to keep your premium lower, consider having higher deductibles and lower limits. Make sure you can afford the deductible in case you need to cover it if something unexpected happens to your truck.

4. **Make advance annual payments** – This refers to when you make your annual insurance payments in advance as a lump sum which will decrease your premium by 10% to 20% in most cases.

It's advisable that you visit at least three insurance companies or insurance brokers who will assist you in choosing the best fitting coverage for your truck. Regardless of how you purchase your coverage, be it through an agency or broker make sure you get the best costs that are affordable to your business. Ensure that you refer to the many factors that affect premium costs and know what will be required on your end.

Remember that just because one premium is cheaper, that doesn't make it the best decision based on value rather than quality. Buying cheap coverage could also hinder some brokers from working with your trucking company because it creates a sense of insecurity and lack of confidence.

Fuel card services

A fuel card is like a credit card, but it's used by businesses that are involved in transport and fleet management. It allows cash free purchase of fuel at gas stations. Just like normal credit cards, fuel cards involve swiping and entering a PIN number by the user. There are several fuel card companies offering fuel cards as per customers' needs by granting them access to a network of gas stations. Using a fuel card for your trucking company will also save you money.

Types of fuel cards

The following are the types of fuel cards offered:

1. **International** – These are cards that can be used through third-party agreements. Customers can refuel at automatic gas pumps.

2. **Bunkered** – This involves fuel card service providers reserving fuel at a specific gas network for the purpose of offering it at a discount. The customer can save money because the fuel is at a pre-negotiated price despite the rising market price.

3. **Retail** – Customers have the option of refueling at any gas station across the nation.

4. **Company** – This card is used by fleets whose main operation is transportation. They're greatly affected by any changes in fuel prices.

All fuel cards being offered by fuel card services have various discounts for their business customers. Most customers compare fuel cards with credit cards. The following are the main differences between the two:

1. Fuel cards offer discounted fuel prices while credit cards do not.

2. Unlike the fuel card, the credit card comes with a greater security risk.

3. One must keep receipts of every transaction when using a credit card which is not the case with fuel cards since it's used for fuel only.

4. Fuel cards have restricted use at networks while credit cards can be used anywhere.

5. Unlike a fuel card, the credit card can't measure efficiency or filling patterns.

Most trucking companies use fuel cards. You should also consider using fuel cards in your business to aid in fuel cost management as well as fuel efficiency.

Benefits of fuel cards

The following are the benefits of fuel cards:

- **Service customization** - Several fuel card providers have applied personalized customization. For example, one customer service employee will be assigned to serve the same company, making it easier to identify the companies' needs.

- **Single invoicing** – Fuel card management has eliminated the need of drivers having to collect several receipts or invoices for the purpose of administrative handling. The fuel card companies provide a single invoice with summarized fueling history. Depending on the package, these invoices are sent weekly or monthly.

- **Discounted fuel price** – Cost saving is a great priority for any business. Fuel card companies purchase fuel at prices lower than the stipulated retail price. This is highly beneficial to those large companies who operate a large number of vehicles in their fleet.

- **Easy to use** – Having accessible fuel filling history and costs on a single online platform saves a lot of time and effort by minimizing the otherwise tedious steps that would have to be followed by fleet managers and accounting departments in retrieving that data. It also provides access to extra functions such as the amount of fuel consumed weekly. It also has more sophisticated systems like a database with fueling patterns and fraud alert systems which are sent by text message or email for customer convenience.

- **High-security** – Fuel cards operate on a PIN code and chip technology which encourages drivers not to carry unnecessary cash with them and reduces risky situations while at the same time preventing activities related to fraud.

  Every card is registered to an individual driver or vehicle allowing the tracking of regular patterns and comparing them to averages on databases. Any abnormal activity can be spotted immediately, and relevant people are alerted via text message or mail.

- **More control over expenses** – Company managers can monitor fuel costs and consumption costs incurred by drivers by having personalized reports. This involves having each driver's account set up separately and enabling central control. This also prevents unauthorized purchases.

Fuel card companies are divided into two groups:

Independent – Independent fuel card companies offer an array of different cards irrespective of their brand.

Branded – They are also known as bunkered. These fuel card companies provide cards that can only be used in certain gas stations that are in their network.

Businesses select fuel cards based on various factors such as organizational processes, consumption patterns, and its fleet.

Factors for customer consideration

Below are the factors that customers need to consider when investing in fuel cards:

- **Invoicing option** – As discussed earlier, when operating your trucking business, you will be in a better position to determine your company's accounting system, cash flow, and other administrative activities. The fuel card company will be able to send your billing either weekly, monthly or even quarterly as per your request which is based on your needs
- **Availability of personalized customer service** – The fuel card company should have an assigned customer service agent that handles all your queries

and meets all of your business's needs.

- **Single network versus a range of gas station networks** – Depending on your trucking company's needs, you should be able to decide whether a single network of gas stations or a gas station network is best for you.

- **Discount program** – Every fuel card comes with the added perk of pre-negotiated discounts.

- **Level of security** – Fuel cards don't carry high-security risks like credit cards do, offering you a better option for your business.

It's important to note that some fuel card companies provide fuel cards for free and all that is required is a certain minimum usage in a specific timeframe.

Some companies charge fees based on the payment plan and network coverage. The approximate cost of a single fuel card ranges from $7.65 to $31.87 annually.

How to purchase a fuel card

Purchasing a fuel card is a simple and fast process because you will just need to access the website of your preferred fuel card service provider where you can fill in your personal information. When applying for fuel cards a customer is required to have the following information:

1. Bank account details
2. Full business details

3. Vehicle and driver's information

After filling in the form online, the rest is taken care of by the fuel card company on their end. Usually, a customer is contacted soon after the application is processed with a business package proposition that is tailored to meet the customer's needs.

It's advisable that you contact the fuel card company for assistance before you choose how you want to use the fuel card since it can be an overwhelming task.

Management Software

Management software is a software designed to automate and streamline management processes for the purpose of reducing the complex task of operations. When you get into the trucking business, you'll typically encounter the following paperwork:

1. Dispatch records
2. Driver pay records
3. Invoices
4. Interstate Fuel Tax Agreement (IFTA) reports and payments
5. Truck maintenance records
6. Mileage reports
7. Expense records

8. Management reports (such as expenses per mile or profit per mile)

All of these must be filled in correctly and must be free of errors to prevent tax penalties. Manually tracking your trucks, planning routes, answering calls from customers, etc. would involve a lot of time and potentially costly human errors. This can be avoided with an efficient management system.

Trucking companies need a reliable dispatch management strategy for successful operations. By employing a management software into your operations, it will give you time to focus on other strategic aspects of the trucking business which include more efficient ways of providing your services. This will also enhance the employees' productivity.

Dispatch Software

This is the software that is used in the trucking industry. A dispatch software will help by automating the routing and scheduling processes thereby enabling coordination of routes and efficient deliveries by your trucking company.

For manufacturing companies, merging the supply chain management software with transport and logistics solutions helps improve the process of sourcing raw materials. It reduces the time spent on making products and eventually delivering them to customers.

The leading software providers usually offer a logistics module which assists with the maintenance of vehicles, routing or mapping, fuel costs, and warehousing, among other important features.

Benefits of a Dispatch Software

Dispatch software will have a great impact on your trucking business. Below are some of the benefits:

- **Management of transportation**

Management software makes it possible to have absolute control over every transportation and mobile employees' processes. It allows tracking of your team's location and status in the field using tools like GPS (Global Positioning System), allowing control over when and where you can dispatch your employees.

It will be improving your team's routes as well as consistency in the quality of services rendered to your customers.

- **Quick response**

In the trucking business, there are many things that can go wrong on the road. Since it's not a guarantee that things will run smoothly every day, a dispatch software is crucial for spotting and tracking incidents, providing you with real-time data on the location and status of your employees.

- **Flexibility**

The more your business grows, the more complicated the dispatch process is, which could lead to errors if there is a lack of proper systems in place to prevent them.

Dispatch software solutions are designed for flexibility. They can manage scheduling and dispatching ensuring each load is delivered to the client on time. It can also be made unique to meet your specific needs.

Essential Features of a Dispatch Management Software

The following are the most important features of a dispatch management software:

- **GPS Tracking and Mapping**

A reliable GPS tracking and mapping function are important because a dispatch software relies on tracking the location and status of each employee. It gives access to real-time data, such as the current traffic conditions. Having this data makes it easier for your employees to identify the best possible routes to ensure a timely delivery of services. It also enables easy navigation through unknown areas through the integration of a map service.

- **Automated scheduling**

A trucking business needs to automate manual tasks to enable effectiveness. A dispatch software will comfortably allow you to handle tasks that run concurrently, like monitoring business growth while tracking scheduled jobs, customers that need to be served, and available technicians.

A dispatch software makes it possible to manage your employees' schedules quickly and easily. It also enables you to assign multiple tasks in an instant.

You'll be able to identify the right technician for each job. The technicians will also take less time in making repairs since the dispatch software provides them with most of the necessary information.

- **Mobile access**

In the trucking business, drivers who are mobile employees

need an accessible and convenient communication channel. Dispatch software comes with mobile apps which allows the drivers to receive any necessary information and quickly respond to the office.

A two-way communication channel is established, allowing employees in the office to communicate with drivers and technicians about any arising issues.

Drivers can reduce the time it would take to complete paperwork. This is possible since the mobile app enables them to have control over their trips and access relevant route information while automatically collecting and storing data of their progress. In turn, errors are greatly minimized.

- **Automated notifications**

As your trucking business grows, automated notifications will come in handy since it will be difficult to keep up with all the progress as it happens in real-time.

Some of the tools offered by fuel card companies work by automatically notifying dispatchers of trips that may fail to meet their delivery schedule, spotting issues with scheduling days in advance. This information helps with proactively solving issues with a few clicks as opposed to trying to fix problems as they occur or after they occur.

This software also helps in tracking each driver's performance, making it possible to identify the areas of performance that need improvement.

- **Convenient invoicing**

The software eliminates the time-consuming process of invoicing while in the field by streamlining it and considerably minimizing the time it takes.

It can also track every expense, from equipment to labor while at the same time successfully sorting out rates and customers' discounts if there are any.

When it comes to the technicians, the software enables the collection of payments from credit cards, offering a convenient billing and payment system that results in customer satisfaction.

How to choose Dispatch Software

Many of the leading dispatch software comes with a variety of features that could make it overwhelming for someone just starting their trucking company to make the right choice. How do you find the best software fit for your trucking company?

This will depend on your priorities. For a startup with a single truck or two, your decision will be based on the price. When this is the case, it eliminates some software service providers based on your budget. Your trucking company can choose a less expensive option that provides the key functions needed to operate your business.

For those with more experience, you will need to look beyond the budget in order to maximize the value of the software solution as opposed to the cost.

As a startup, it's important to know that just because there is a cheaper solution that doesn't mean that it's going to be worth it. It might be incapable of meeting the needs of your trucking company or it could be unadaptable as the business grows.

Cheap can sometimes mean expensive. If you have to change

systems and start from scratch, it can ultimately be more expensive to your business. Not to mention the losses that your trucking business could incur if the initial system fails to meet the business projections.

At the same time, just because a software system is expensive, that doesn't guarantee that it's efficient for your business. Even the most expensive software solutions can have issues like unreliability, poor support, or they may be missing key functions needed by your trucking company.

In order to increase your return on investment, the following are a few questions that will assist in narrowing down your list:

- **What features are most important for your company?**

Dispatch software comes with a variety of features and not all software service providers have the solutions you need since they all vary.

It's important for you to establish the features that will be of most value to your company. By so doing, you'll be able to make a number of eliminations from your list of software companies. These features include integrated map services, remote monitoring, and mobile app availability among many others.

- **Does it offer comprehensive training?**

Rigorous training programs should be offered by the software provider to enable your trucking company's employees to utilize it to the maximum extent, which will go a long way in ensuring that you benefit from the software solution.

Not only should these trainings equip the employees with the knowledge to operate the software, but it should also offer substantial support in case the need of additional features comes up in the future.

It's advisable to try the demo version of the solution and see if it's compatible with your business's needs.

- **How does pricing structure compare with functionality?**

There are different cost structures for different software providers. It's important to determine which provider is within your budget requirements.

For example, depending on the size of your company you may or may not need to get a customizable software. You'll need to determine if the extra cost of that feature will be worth it with where your business is currently at and where it's projected to go.

How to handle logistics in a trucking business

It's important to understand what logistics entail in your trucking business. Simply put, logistics are the efficient storage and flow of goods from their point of origin to the point of consumption in order to meet the customer's requirements. These activities make up the supply chain functions which include transportation, shipping, receiving, storage, and overall management of these activities.

Transportation and logistics have become key factors in the trucking business and should be included while making business plans.

In the trucking business, logistics involve:

- **Inventory** – Inventory involves storage management in terms of having prior knowledge of when goods will be brought for storage, for how long they will be there, and also when they will leave the storage. All these elements pertaining to storage should be easily accessible by maintaining an inventory. Automation and integration become essential as it will minimize the time that will be spent if these things were to be done manually.

- **Fleet management** – It also involves fleet management in terms of knowing the available trucks, their routes and their mileage. This is made possible by employing a GPS system. It's vital to invest in a GPS that will make operations easier to run as discussed earlier in the book. A GPS tracking device will help in running your trucking company both effectively and efficiently since it gives complete remote control of the business without having to be there in-person.

- **Transportation** – This involves having a plan on when the goods are to be moved, where the goods are being moved to, and how they will be moved using the best possible route. Proper planning of your trucking business operations will ensure that the goods are where they're supposed to be as per the customers' orders. Providing good customer service, as well as timely service delivery, are essential to your success.

The logistics involved in transportation include planning on the mode of transport, carrier scheduling, and the weight of your cargo.

Transport involves;

1. **Equipment** - In the trucking business the trucks are the equipment.
2. **People** - The drivers, the loaders, and the unloaders
3. **Decisions** – Decisions on which route to take, the timings of dispatch and delivery, the quantity of cargo to haul, and the mode of transport.

All the above need to be factored in when handling transport costs as they can take up between 1/3 and 2/3 of the total costs.

When it comes to planning the routes, the following should be taken into consideration:

1. Ensure that the load points for the same truck are close together.
2. When creating the routes, start with the point that is farthest away from the warehouse.
3. Always fill the largest truck to capacity first.
4. Ensure that the routes do not cross each other.
5. Teardrop pattern routes should be formed.
6. Plan pick-ups during deliveries as opposed to after every other delivery.

Managing your trucking business logistics is vital for the effectiveness, efficiency, and success of your trucking company.

License and Permit checklist for starting a trucking company

Trucking is one of the industries involved in heavy regulations that must be met. It's vital that you gain knowledge on the several government regulations that need to be met and maintained. This checklist will navigate you through all the necessary steps that will help you acquire the authority to legally operate as an interstate trucking company.

1. Get a Commercial Driver's License (CDL)

Ensure that all your drivers in the trucking company have a valid commercial driver's license. A thorough background check, CDL training, a written permit exam, and driving test are done before obtaining your license. One must be 18 years old to be eligible for a CDL and at least 21 years old to be an interstate truck driver. The testing standards for every state vary. Find out what your state requires by visiting your nearest Department of Motor Vehicles office.

2. Apply for your Federal DOT and Motor Carrier Authority Numbers

For your trucking company to haul cargo in the United States, these numbers are required. The Federal DOT number is used for tracking the safety records and compliance with regulations of your trucking company.

The Motor Carrier (MC) number is also known as the "operating authority" and it helps in identifying the type of trucking business you operate and the goods that you're permitted to haul. Both numbers can be acquired by registering your trucking company with the Federal Motor

Carrier Safety Administration (FMCSA).

Obtaining both your Motor Carrier (MC) and USDOT numbers involve completing the motor carrier identification report (MCS-150) and Safety Certification Application. After the application is filed you will receive your MC and USDOT numbers but your request for authority must be reviewed by the FMCSA. The review includes a "mandated dispute period" where your application will be posted to the Federal Register for 10 business days. This period is aimed at seeking public remark from anyone who might challenge your application for authority.

3. Complete Your Unified Carrier Registration (UCR)

The UCR system is used for the verification of active insurance coverage in every state where a motor carrier operates. USDOT and MC numbers must be used in registering your company. More information is accessible through your state's Department of Transportation website.

4. Get an International Registration Plan (IRP) Tag

An IRP license plate allows your truck to operate in all states and to most Canadian provinces as well. It's issued by your company's home state. An annual renewal fee is required for an IRP license plate. More information is accessible through your home state's Department of Transportation website.

5. Understand Heavy Use Tax Regulations

If your truck weighs 55,000 pounds or more it will be subjected to the federal heavy highway vehicle use tax. It's mandatory to complete and file a 2290 tax form to be able to pay taxes due on your heavy trucks. This is done with the IRS every year.

6. Obtain an International Fuel Tax Agreement (IFTA) Decal

The IFTA Agreement enables the reporting of fuel consumed by trucks, which operate across the 48 contiguous U.S. states and some Provinces in Canada. Your company can have a single fuel license and a quarterly filing of fuel usage for tax return.

7. File a BOC-3 Form

For your trucking company to acquire authority to operate on the interstate, registration of a current BOC-3 form with the Federal Motor Carrier Safety Administration (FMCSA) is required. A person in every state that your company operates in is selected to act as a legal "process agent". For instance, if your company is based in Ohio but someone in New Jersey sues you, you will need an attorney in New Jersey to receive the legal complaint and communicate to you and your local attorney.

8. Get a Standard Carrier Alpha Code (SCAC)

The SCAC is used in the identification of different companies involved in transportation and it's controlled privately. It's a requirement if your trucking company will be involved in hauling military, government, international or intermodal loads.

The United States Department of Transportation (DOT) Regulations

The Department of Transportation (DOT) regulates truck drivers on the total number of hours they can work per day as well as per week. These rules have been put in place to ensure not only the safety of the driver but also the safety of other people on the road. It aims to have well-rested drivers. The following are the regulations in each category:

1. **General hours of service guidelines**

   a) Drivers are limited to 14 hours on duty, but they may only drive for 11 hours.

   b) By their eighth hour of working, drivers must take a mandatory 30-minute break.

   c) While on the 14-hour period, it may not be extended with off duty time for breaks, meals, fuel stops, etc.

   d) Once every 168-hour work week, drivers can restart the 7-day period. This means taking at least 34 consecutive hours off with two consecutive periods of 1 a.m. to 5 a.m.

   e) The work week starts after the last legal reset.

   f) At least 10 hours off duty must be taken before the start of each period.

   g) In seven consecutive days, drivers may work no more than 60 hours on duty.

2. **16-hour exception**

   h) For one-day work schedules, the 16-hour exception is

designed in a way that the driver begins and ends at the same terminal.

i) You're not allowed to exceed 11 hours of drive time.

j) A driver can't use the Adverse Driving conditions and the 16-hour exception at the same time.

k) The 16-hour exception can't be used if the driver has a layover on any day, including the day of the layover.

l) Until a driver has had a 34-hour reset, then he/she may not use the 16-hour exception more than once.

m) When on duty, drivers may not drive past the 16th hour.

3. Adverse driving conditions exception

n) In case a driver can't complete the run safely within the 11 hours maximum driving time, the driver is allowed an additional 2 hours to reach a destination. Nevertheless, the driver may not drive past the 14th hour on duty.

o) If weather conditions force the driver to pull over at a hotel or rest stop for 10 hours off duty, two hours of drive time may be extended by the driver.

p) This exception does not mean that due to bad weather the driver can work longer. If within an 11-hour drive a driver can stop safely and layover, they're required to do so, provided they can't make it back to their terminal within 14 hours or under the 16-hour exception if available.

4. 34-hour restart

q) The 60/70 calculation will be restarted at any period of 34 consecutive hours off duty.

r) Two periods of 1 a.m. to 5 p.m. must be included in the restart. Once per 168-hour week, the drivers are allowed to use the 34-hour restart.

5. Penalties for violating hours of service rules

s) Until the driver has accumulated enough time to be back in compliance, drivers may be placed on shutdown which is at the roadside.

t) Fines may be assessed by the state and local law enforcement officials.

u) Civil penalties ranging from $1,000 to $11,000 per violation may be levied on drivers or carriers by the FMCSA.

v) For a pattern of violations, the carrier's safety rating can be downgraded.

w) Federal criminal penalties may be imposed upon carriers who willfully and knowingly allow or require HOS violations; or drivers who knowingly and willfully violate the HOS regulations.

Handling audits

To be able to know how to go about audits, it's important to know what an audit is and who performs them.

Auditing is the process of evaluating and diagnosing the

financial and operational activities of an organization to determine if they're complying with the official regulations. It's conducted by an authorized state agency.

Documentation is the key to any audit compliance. We'll go over the several types of (FMCSA) Federal Motor Carrier Safety Administration audits and discuss a corrective action plan in case any faults are found during the audit.

FMCSA Audit

This audit assesses the safety performance and determines the proper and complete recordkeeping of your trucking company. In order to ensure compliance with regulations, the review conducted also determines if the company has sufficient management controls in place. If your trucking company understands the regulations that they're subject to and the records expected by the Department of Transportation (DOT) then they can have an easier time during the audit. By demonstrating a gross lack of compliance, an audit can subject your company to hefty fines.

An FMCSA safety audit entails the assessment of seven BASIC (Behavior Analysis Safety Improvement Categories) factors to determine if the carrier is in compliance with the safety regulations and lend a hand in establishing a solid safety program. The seven BASICs are as follows:

a) crash indicator

b) Vehicle maintenance

c) Hours of service

d) Controlled substance and alcohol

e) Driver fitness

f) Unsafe driving

g) And HAZMAT, if your company carries Hazardous Materials

Your company's safety audit will be conducted by either a Federal DOT Officer or by a state agency on behalf of the Federal DOT.

Since the audit will be safety related the focus will be on the things that directly affect the company's ability to safely operate commercial vehicles on the road.

Some of the different types of documents that are included in the DOT Audit are:

1. A driver's hours of service

2. Vehicle maintenance and inspection

3. Driver qualification files

4. Drug and alcohol testing

5. Commercial driver license requirements

6. Accidents

7. Safety management controls

The above list, however, does not contain all the documents as there are many others that could be involved.

Now let's dive into the different types of DOT audits your trucking company could be subjected to.

Types of *DOT Audits*

FMCSA New Entrant Audit

Being a new entrant into the trucking business, your company will be required to go through a detailed DOT safety compliance audit within the first 12 months of operation, as the DOT will expect to see some set processes and records. The safety audit will not usually be done until the carrier has been in operation for at least six months.

There are sixteen key audit areas in which non-compliance with any one of them in a new entrant audit will result in failing the audit and could, in turn, cancel your company's operating authority.

This audit may be conducted in person with a DOT officer or it may be online through an audit upload which involves you uploading the required documentation directly to the FMCSA website. After the New Entrant audit period, there are a few different types of Compliance reviews.

FMCSA Comprehensive Compliance Review

A safety audit or compliance review is an assessment of a motor carrier's records in all classifications of safety compliance by a safety investigator from the FMCSA. Any motor carrier can be singled out at any given time for a compliance review, but generally, they're singled out due to multiple safety basics being exceeded as a result of a complaint or accident involving your company's trucks. This audit culminates into determining and issuing a motor carrier with a safety fitness classification as either satisfactory, conditional or unsatisfactory.

FMCSA Focused Review

The DOT will usually conduct a focused review when only one of your safety basics has exceeded its limits or when routinely following up after a compliance review was performed to ensure there is evidence that corrections have taken place. During the focused review, the DOT auditor will only review the area of concern that has been identified, and the auditor requires only the records that support your compliance in that specific area.

This review can be conducted both off-site and on-site. The review does not result in a safety rating but could be stipulated as impossible to rate and possibly incur fines in the event that a major non-compliance is discovered.

DOT's Hazardous Materials Review and Security Review

A HAZMAT review is a very rigorous review of requirements related to transporting hazardous materials, such as training, shipping papers, policies, placards, markings, and labeling of containers.

The security review includes a security plan, training, and other security-associated procedures. Usually, security reviews accompany a HAZMAT review if the company transports hazardous materials.

Corrective Action Plan

Once the FMCSA has assigned a less than satisfactory safety rating or lowered a current rating, in addition to heavy fines, the upgrading process is time-consuming as it usually takes months and many hours of work.

It's important to know that a carrier assigned an unsatisfactory rating has 60 days to salvage the business by proving to the FMCSA that its defects have been dealt with or face an out-of-service order.

When the DOT steps in to correct a safety problem, they will usually require a detailed response, in writing, informing them of the corrective actions you have put into place. The FMCSA takes 45 days out of those 60 days to review the CAP and to establish if the grading can be moved up to conditional.

To avoid being shut down, an unsatisfactory graded carrier has only 15 days to execute and document a successful corrective action plan.

Truck maintenance

The vehicle maintenance BASIC guides on the Federal Motor Carrier Safety Regulations are requirements intended to help the prevention of shifting of loads, spilling, or dropping of cargo and the overloading of a commercial motor vehicle.

The safety officers inspect trucks for any safety defects which include:

- Leaking or wet wheel seals
- A discharged fire extinguisher
- Broken or worn suspensions
- Broken windshield wipers
- Loose ball joints or evidence of worn kingpins

The above list does not contain all the possible defects that there could be because there are many more defects that can occur.

The safety officers also subject trucks to a roadside inspection where they inspect the brakes, lights, and tires. These three things are the cause of most violations by motor vehicles and taking care of them will improve your BASIC Maintenance.

If the DOT investigator conducts the "in office" inspection, some of the vital documents needed are vehicle maintenance files, inspection reports, accidents reports, roadside inspection reports, annual vehicle inspection reports, and evidence of driver training on load securement. Always ensure that these documents are well organized and easily accessible. The safety officers usually use these documents to determine the severity of a safety violation by your trucking company.

Ensure that your truck drivers and maintenance technicians in your trucking company are trained on the maintenance program in order to improve on the BASIC maintenance.

Negotiation of Freight Rates

Most startups in the trucking business face the major challenge of freight negotiation to their customers. Small trucking companies, unlike large carriers, lack adequate resources and as a result, they're less advantaged compared to large carriers.

The following are tips for negotiating:

- **Small carriers structural work up**

When rates are paid according to a percentage on the basis of the gross load, small trucking businesses find it quite difficult to negotiate. Lower rates will eventually reduce your business profits, but you can improve your negotiation ability. Your business can go about this by going through their organizational structures and having each department chip in for freight rate to prospective customers.

- **Improving the performance of the pricing department**

The pricing department is charged with the responsibility of communicating with your target market. This communication aims to inform people about the cost of your services. In order to determine the correct freight charges, it's vital to consider all your costs of operation which includes salaries, insurance costs, tax liabilities, truck maintenance costs, and fuel expenses.

By having these costs, your business knows the level below which it can't go hence making negotiation easier. This will mostly come in handy when your customers ask for discounts hence having a baseline cost will guide you on whether to accept or turn them down.

- **Building business relationships with brokers, shippers, and clients**

Building business relationships will enable your trucking company to accept and turn down some freight offers from the same broker or shipper. It's vital to communicate your expectations to your clients or brokers from the onset so that you don't come off as offensive if you turn down their offered freight charges. By communicating, they will be in a position to understand your cost factors hence making it easier to negotiate your rates that they will hopefully find reasonable.

As long as your company is known for its excellent customer service and up to date trucking logistics, selling your services will not be difficult. In fact, because of your top-notch services customers will pursue your rates. Combine reliability and honesty in your trucking services and you will achieve a track record that will make it easier to negotiate your freight rates with brokers and shippers.

- **Instill flexibility into your freight rate**

Even though large carriers have the capability of handling more cargo, it's impossible to meet all the demands of shipping services. These gaps are where small carriers add value to the trucking industry by meeting the demands from various industries.

Making your freight rate highly flexible will help you gain more revenue for your trucking business. By doing this, customers will find your services to be more satisfying, allowing you to gain regular clients.

Applying the above tips should enable you to be in a position to negotiate for the best trucking jobs.

Chapter 5: How to Hire Winning Employees that Will Exponentially Grow Your Business

Most trucking businesses start as owner-operators who are involved in every part of the business from taking customer orders, to accounting, to marketing, and many other roles. Eventually, your business will grow, and you'll need to employ other staff for you to concentrate on more strategic plans.

This chapter will teach you how to hire the right employees by walking you through the steps involved. You'll have the confidence you need in making decisions regarding your prospective staff.

Hiring the wrong employee is costly to your work environment, and time-consuming whereas hiring the right employee will pay you back in employee productivity, a successful employment relationship, and a positive impact on your overall work environment.

So many mistakes are made when hiring. Most new entrants into the world of business have the assumption that you can pick employees using the traditional ways that have always been applied.

Hiring employees involves conducting thorough interviews that will help match what you are really looking for in a candidate. The quality of the people you employ will not only get the job done but they will also have an impact on company culture as well as the company's financial worth. Before we look at the importance, we will cover the things to consider when hiring. They are as follows:

1. Focus on the person

Focusing on the person addresses the importance of a candidate's social intelligence, which is how well that person interacts with others. It basically helps employers to focus on the candidate's personality as opposed to just meeting the job qualifications. Companies can teach new skills through training but they cannot teach on acquiring new personalities.

You could start by identifying the most important character traits that you are looking for and then build a list of related questions. By doing so the interview will turn into a conversation which can reveal how they will be in terms of organizational skills, ability to be trained, transparency and humility.

The personality should not only match the company but also the job since different job functions need different personalities which will go a long way in contributing to the company's success.

2. The ability to learn

With the development of new technology and business processes, job responsibilities and tasks also change often. Part of evaluation on the part of the employers should be how well and fast the candidate learns new things.

3. How they answer probing questions

Being ready to probe further when particular responses to

interview questions are given is one way of getting a view of the candidate's personality. For instance, let's say a candidate is asked about his or her reason for leaving his or her previous job.

The response the candidate gives points the reason at a manager or colleague. This suggests that this candidate is shifting the blame to someone else.

Upon getting such a response the employer should ask more questions that could lead to the candidate pointing fingers at others whether it is the whole answer or just a part of it. Employers should take this as a warning sign if it emerges to be a pattern.

4. Allowing them to demonstrate their skills

The entire hiring process is a test. The candidates who demonstrate transparency, humility, desire, and organizational skills will always stand out. This technique will help weed out those who do not demonstrate these qualities. This will help to avoid making big mistakes when it comes to hiring.

5. Understand what they are really looking for

As much as every person wants to get paid, it is not the key to making the right candidates happy. You need to know what's in it for the potential candidate because satisfying an individual's motivators is the best way of retaining a good employee.

6. Long-term growth and potential

When looking at potential employees, it is also important to factor in their potential growth within the company. You should be able to project the employee lifecycle.

Like stated earlier just because their skills are written on paper that does not mean that they are actually capable of accomplishing the job at hand. Do not be under the impression that just because the candidate has the right experience, he or she is right for the job.

You should try to find out if he or she has any other skills apart from those required for the job. It is important to know if the candidate can solve problems because it will mean that he or she will not need to be constantly guided.

The candidate will be in a good position to take direction and make successful decisions. Find out if he or she has any leadership skills that will propel him or her to a higher position and whether he or she will strive to do more than just what he or she is asked to do.

All of this knowledge will help you to know how long the person will last in the company.

Effects of a Bad Hire

The cost of a bad hire will cost you in a variety of ways. The most common are:

· Less productivity

· Lost time to recruit and train another worker

· Cost to recruit and train another worker

· Employee morale will negatively be affected

· Negative impact on clients

· Fewer sales

· Possible legal issues

Importance of hiring the right employees

According to the U.S. Department of Labor, the cost of a bad hire stands at about 30% of the annual salary for that position. Below are the benefits of hiring the right employee:

You will minimize the cost of the hiring process

It is a known fact that the process of hiring is very expensive. Not only does it require you to take time out of your already busy schedule but you will also spend money on job postings, skill tests, criminal background checks and much more.

Whenever you end up hiring the wrong person, you will have to conduct the same hiring process all over again hence doubling the cost. Hiring the right employee will eliminate the need for a second hiring process as well as the added cost.

You will maximize productivity

Time is valuable hence conducting a hiring process means you and your team will leave your daily routines to review applications and conduct interviews. When you conduct several interviews every day for a few weeks, it starts to get difficult to finish your other work. A fast and rigorous hiring process will allow you to get back to your work sooner and with enhanced productivity.

You will save time

Time spent reviewing applications and conducting interviews will be saved. When you spend most of your time going through the hiring process, you lose interest due to the monotony of it all.

This might cause you to miss out on the recognition of a good candidate. You will find that every resume looks about the same.

The hiring process should occur less often and further apart to enable you and your hiring team to be refreshed. Having a clear head gives you an easier time for when you have to hire again.

Saves you from potential damage

For a lot of different reasons, bad hires can have a negative impact on your company. Some could be a safety risk to customers and colleagues hence the reason for conducting criminal background checks.

A bad hire might ruin your company's reputation and jeopardize your client relations by being incompetent among so many other things. Bad hires almost always damage your business in some way. Avoiding a bad hire means you will not have to deal with any such potential damages.

You will preserve the morale of your internal teams

A good hire not only comes with new skills and experience to your team but can also bring inspiration, warmth, and togetherness to your company culture. On the other hand, a bad hire could hurt your entire team's morale by causing harm to the work culture through a bad attitude or being a joyrider or a bully.

You will protect your image as an employer

When your company culture goes bad, the news will always spread outside. For instance, let's say your employees keep leaving because they are not happy with their jobs anymore, and they say negative things about your business.

These things will give a poor reflection of you and your company such that other people will not want to join your team. Hiring the right people, however, will always protect your reputation.

You won't let the good candidates leave

Hiring someone means having to turn down dozens of other applicants. A good number of those who have been let go are probably qualified for that position.

If you happen to get the right employee, losing the rest won't hurt as much. However, when you make a bad hire, it can be so annoying to know that you let better candidates go.

By the time you realize this most of them will probably have found other jobs or they would not be so keen to come back to a place where they already faced rejection.

You don't have to train an employee who won't stick around

The entire hiring process is quite a struggle, but usually the biggest annoyance is employee onboarding. Helping new employees to blend in, training them and familiarizing them with your company's processes and policies usually takes a lot of time.

Despite how talented or adaptable the person is, the process of onboarding does not happen overnight. It could take your new hire months if not a year, depending on the level of the position.

Investing all that time and effort into someone who is not going to be a part of your company's long-term future is the greatest blow of making a bad hire. That's not even to mention the fact that you will also have to go through the entire process of onboarding again.

You avoid giving passwords and confidential company information to people you cannot trust.

Nowadays every employee needs access to company software, accounts, websites, and other confidential information. It is not an issue to give out this information because normally, you are giving it to people who will be a part of the company for a long time.

However, when you bring in a bad hire and give them access to your company only to terminate their contract a few months later, you are at risk of cybersecurity.

As much as the IT team can remove the user's accounts, software licenses, and logins, you cannot erase what that person came across while working in your company. By hiring the right person from the onset, a limited number of people will ever be granted access to your company's data and systems.

What to Look For In Good Employees

Good employees are recognized through the qualities they possess. It is paramount as an employer to identify the qualities of good employees since they are an asset to your company.

Retaining good employees is also quite challenging. You will want to hire good employees who will stay for a long time. Without putting the entire emphasis on personality, there are other distinct qualities to look for irrespective of the age or gender of the candidate. They are as follows:

a) Ambitious

For the purpose of achieving company goals or climbing the corporate ladder, ambitious employees are always willing to go the extra mile. They will give their very best because they set goals and high expectations for themselves.

They also strive to advance in their career. Ambition activates creative ideas, openness and a go-getter attitude, which are good for your company. Your ambitious candidate should, however, have a reasonable amount of emotional intelligence. This will ensure that he or she does not isolate most of his or her workmates.

b) Confident

As the owner in your trucking business startup, it will obviously make you happier handing a project over to a confident person as opposed to a doubtful person. A confident person will be willing to take on the challenge and the risks that come with it, all of which the uncertain person would shy away from. People who believe in themselves have a great outcome. If you were to let a candidate interact directly with a client, they would be impressed by the confident person which would encourage them to continue the business relationship.

c) Humble

People do not like those who brag about their achievements. The preferable candidate should be someone who is capable of proving himself/herself through their hard and admirable work as opposed to just words. Arrogant employees do not belong in a productive workplace.

d) Passionate

Every employer is drawn to an employee who is always

willing to do more than just what is required of him or her and that means getting involved in things that are not in his or her line of duty. This is the kind of person who continually surpasses expectations and gladly accepts any task or project, however challenging it may be.

Furthermore, a passionate person will not feel like he or she is working because he or she loves what he or she does. The time he or she spends at work with his or her colleagues and superiors is so fulfilling to him or her.

Despite money being a motivator, people working for you should seem to be enjoying what they do to get paid. There are two questions that you can ask in an interview to identify if the candidate is a passionate person:

a) At your last place of employment, what was it about your work that made you feel the most satisfied?

The candidate's answer to this question will tell you if the person is looking to apply his or her passion into his or her work, or if he or she is just looking for a comfortable place of work.

b) How do you stay informed about your industry?

As far as passion is concerned, it will definitely be a red flag if the candidate is unable to mention any recent development he or she has done whether positive or negative. Passionate people spend any extra time they have sharpening their skills and acquiring new knowledge. The genuine candidate will have enthusiasm showing in his or her eyes.

e) Reliable

There aren't many things that are more irritating to deal with than an employee who does not follow instructions. It shows that either he or she is not serious or he or she fails in listening to instructions attentively.

The obvious result of such behavior is making mistakes, not meeting deadlines, faulty products and of course disappointed or unhappy clients. An employee who does not listen until the entire instructions are given and also keeps interrupting shows a lack of respect to his boss.

By following instructions an employee shows that he takes his work seriously and is even capable of taking up extra responsibility. Additionally, a reliable employee will show up to work on time, inform the relevant authorities if he cannot make it and meets deadlines.

This type of employee has a greater chance to stick around the company for a while.

f) Positive

Most people do not like being around those who are negative, pessimistic or just unhappy. One should always be optimistic and happy no matter what they are going through.

Happiness and positivity are infectious hence the workplace will be full of happy people. Regardless of how monotonous or menial the given task is, a positive person will perform his or her duties happily and efficiently.

Additionally, employers feel good when they get employees who are able to identify problems and are willing to offer solutions. The more problem-solving skills they prove to have, the more valuable they are to the company. This kind of employee will bring you closer to realizing your company's goals.

To identify a positive candidate during the interview, you should ask questions like:

With examples can you mention one or two things that you are optimistic about in life?

g) Culturally fit

It can be difficult to find a candidate that matches your company's culture. To ensure that you get the best fit, first start by having a clear idea of what your company's culture is. Then think about the values and characteristics of potential employees that you may hire and see if it lines up with you and your company's values. To find a candidate that fits into your company culture, you could ask any of the following questions:

- With examples name three of your work-related values.
- Have ever made a mistake? If yes tell us how you fixed the problem.

When you find a candidate who is a match for your company culture, you should ensure that you offer them lucrative compensation packages, motivating leadership opportunities or chances of having a direct role in projects.

h) Self-motivated/ Driven

You will not have to push self-motivated people to get work done. They continually work hard and always produce outstanding work. With a self-driven employee, you will not have to worry about wasted time or having a lazy worker. They encourage others to copy their example. They have a great return on investment as they do not require any additional rewards.

Self-motivated individuals know their purpose in life and they are always able to rise above problems, loss, adversity and momentary failure. They believe in themselves as well as others. They embody humility and can even laugh at themselves, take criticism positively and admit when they are wrong. They regularly keep updating their knowledge and are very determined.

i) Enthusiastic

People who portray enthusiasm and energy every day have an advantage over their workmates who are not as enthusiastic hence they easily burn out. Employees who are eager with a lot of liveliness are always excited to learn new things and they aim for greater success. They contribute to making the work environment enjoyable and unique to their workmates. They also create an environment where new ideas are born regularly.

j) Hardworking

The benefits of hard work are irreplaceable. Some people work hard for a few years then they lose the psyche. Some people who specifically work from 9 to 5 can't exactly be considered to be hard working in a certain sense.

These people typically won't stay late or be willing to go the extra mile in order to get the job done. They'll do the minimum that's required of them. Hiring result oriented and industrious employees can greatly change the overall effectiveness of an organization. Such employees constantly remind themselves and the company of how important it is to keep working hard.

k) Team spirit

Most companies work in teams. Not only is it vital to work well individually but also as a team member. Performing well in a team takes good social skills, patience, and tolerance. Team efforts come with various advantages like when more people are involved in a project the work gets done faster, employee relationships are improved and team members learn from each other's feedback.

l) Self –managed

Employers do not like employees who have to be told what is expected of them but rather those who know what is expected of them and are even willing to go the extra mile. Additionally, a self-managed employee is aware of his or her duties and roles needed to improve himself or herself.

This allows him or her to make use of his or her strengths and minimize his or her weaknesses. Most self-managed employees are also self-disciplined hence they will not waste work time on distractions like their cellphone or browsing the internet. This kind of employee is diligent, always punctual and does not take unnecessary breaks or procrastinate.

m) Proactive

There are those employees who are reactive and there are those who are proactive. The reactive employees are the ones who have to be told what to do, whereas the proactive employees will take the initiative of trying to be more productive by being innovative. A proactive person always thinks ahead and executes without waiting to be requested to do so. This kind of employee stands out and is easily noticeable.

Moreover, strive to hire those who are willing to show

initiative and take chances. Taking chances of course have a possibility of failure but failure offers a learning experience from which success is achieved. These are the employees who demonstrate confidence and bring new ideas to the table. They are also the employees that generate the most money for your company.

n) Marketable

The right employee should also be presentable to clients a.k.a. marketable. This employee should positively represent your company by painting a picture of the company's values to the clients.

By so doing he or she should be able to give potential clients the confidence they need to feel good about working with your company. Additionally, this person should have a great personality and demonstrate professionalism.

o) Detail-oriented

Paying great attention to detail is critical as it eliminates the likelihood of making any unnecessary mistakes. An employee who is able to pay attention to every detail is always proud of his or her work. He or she will apply more effort without taking minor details for granted.

p) Autonomous

Autonomy means giving employees the freedom to plan their work and execute it their own way. An autonomous employee will be able to deliver without having to inquire about everything that needs to be done from you since you also have a lot of work to do.

This kind of employee does not need supervision and will always deliver on projects delegated to him or her since he or she is a good time manager and very productive.

q) Creative

Creative employees come up with great ideas since they try out new things and always think outside the box. They therefore help in minimizing redundancy and monotony of the job, which in turn increases the employees' productivity.

r) Honest

Apart from an employee having the rest of these good qualities, the most important quality is someone who is genuine and has integrity. Straightforward employees also attract customer relations hence more growth for your company as a result of customer satisfaction.

An honest employee is transparent, which enhances the company culture thereby making every employee in the workplace have a sense of joy. Moreover, you will appreciate having honest and humble people in your company's management.

s) Communicator

It is of great value to have employees who are capable of communicating eloquently. Poor communication skills could be harmful to any organization. It also involves an employee knowing what to say, how to say it, when to say it and whom to say it to. Inappropriate or inaccurate communication among employees could lead to internal disputes or even create problems with clients.

t) Has leadership qualities

An employee who portrays leadership has self-confidence. This person will also be successful with any given task. This is the person you could consider assigning some leadership role to in your company.

Characteristics of a Bad Hire

When classifying what makes someone a bad hire, employers reported several behavioral and performance-related issues which are as follows:

· Employee didn't produce the proper quality of work

· Employee didn't work well with other employees

· Employee had a negative attitude

· Employee had immediate attendance problems

· Customers complained about the employee

· Employee didn't meet deadlines

Your company's work culture is enhanced by hiring the right employees. This person will pay you back a thousand times over in high employee morale, positive forward thinking, planning, and accomplishing challenging goals.

It also ensures that you're making the most of the time and energy that your other employees invest in a relationship with the new employee. So, what makes you good at hiring?

To hire the right people you need to establish who you are as an organization, make it clear what you want from your employees, and determine the exact process you'll go through to see if someone is the right fit for your company.

It's not an easy task having to choose the right personality for your organization. You want to choose the employee that best fits the needs of your organization and the target position(s). You can spend weeks sifting through different pre-employment assessments and ask questions like:

- Which will give us the most knowledge about our candidates?

- Which test can best predict performance?

- Which one gives us the most useful information?

- At what point is the assessment too long?

One common mistake that people make is to believe that the assessment that measures the most competencies is the best option. In this case, less is more, the large tests with plenty of dimensions are not as useful as tests with fewer dimensions. These tests will show you the most important information you need, which will save you time.

When determining which personality assessment is the right one for your company, you should look for:

- How well each question is able to predict performance in the target position. In other words, how relevant is each question to the job at hand?

- Ensure that you keep the candidate in mind and that the assessment is not unnecessarily long. Candidates will likely provide accurate information about themselves.

The first step of the hiring process is to figure out how to attract the right applicants and potential employees. How do you do this? You can attract the right employees by doing the following:

1. **Build an inclusive culture** – If you're planning to

bring in talent from younger generations you need to realize how important the work environment is to their motivation and happiness. The younger generation has a different set of values than previous generations. Some adjustments to traditional office structures are required in order to build a work environment that the millennial generation can thrive in. You might need to focus more on technology and technological advances to better utilize them. Hiring young employees also opens your mind up to new ways and methods of operations that may help you find a niche in the trucking market. By giving them what they want, you will be given what you want. You might have to spend more time investing in your environment. You might need to employ the democratic style of leadership. Eventually, you will find yourself adjusting with your employees.

2. **Focus on the future** – As people keep dreaming about who they can become given their potential, everyone is looking for a fulfilling career. They can only achieve this at the company that gives them a chance to do so. People who are motivated to grow, learn new skills, and tackle new challenges, are the right candidates. They will want a company that provides them with an opportunity to learn, prove themselves, be rewarded, and eventually grow. The wrong candidates are just looking for any kind of job. If you fail to convince the right people that you're the right company for their needs, they'll probably take another offer. When you grant them the opportunity of asking questions, you're able to answer them with clarity. Tell them about your goals, your journey up to where you are, your growth projections, and recent

promotions. Tell them about the growth opportunities that are available by using a story about someone in your organization that achieved what they wanted as a practical example. Help them visualize their role and unique contribution as the company grows and you'll cast a vision that they want to be a part of.

After you have drawn this out and have taken care of all the pre-interview points stated above, the next step is to take a look at the interview questions. It's pertinent that you ask the correct questions to get the correct answers.

Don't over script your interview. Be prepared to enjoy the answers and simply have a conversation with your candidate, rather than an interrogation.

The candidate should be at ease and calm with the interview. It's best to narrow it down to a select number of questions to keep the interview short and precise. Allow the candidate ample time to answer and expound on these questions. Here are some examples of questions that you could ask:

1. **Tell us about yourself** – Let the candidate highlight their skills and give you insight into how they perceive themselves.

2. **When was the last time you made a mistake at work and how did you handle it?** - This gives you room to see whether the candidates acknowledge that they can make mistakes and also see if they can take initiative to correct those mistakes.

3. **Where do you see yourself in the next 5 years?** – This question is tried and true and its important because you want to know that the candidate has a clear vision for himself or herself. Look for a

candidate that wants to progress within a structured framework.

4. **Why do you want to work for this company?** – Does the candidate have knowledge about the company? Does his or her skills match the needs of the company? What is he or she bringing in with him or her that sets him or her apart from the rest of the candidates?

5. **Tell us about a time when you had to deliver in a tight deadline** – This is an open-ended question that will reveal a few things for you. First, it will show whether the candidate is able to work under pressure and how he or she reacts to it. Secondly, it will address the subject of working past regular hours, and it will show you some insight into how well the candidate works with other people.

6. **Do you have any questions?** - The questions the candidate has about the company, the ethos, the working conditions, and day-to-day operations can reveal more about their character and commitment than the rest of the interview can.

By the time you get to this point, there's usually one or two candidates who clearly stand out as the most qualified for the job. However, it's surprising that most interviewers change their mind once they have an opportunity to carefully discuss and consider all of the candidates. Be sure to apply an approach that is methodical and consistent in selecting the best candidate for the job.

5 basic steps to improve your selection process

1. Define the job clearly and precisely.

Describe the most crucial tasks of the job and write down your description with specifics about the essential tasks. Also, note how well the tasks must be performed and the level of performance that you expect. For example is this job position going to be an entry-level, intermediate or advanced position?

2. Identify your selection criteria.

Identify the skills needed to carry out these essential job tasks, the knowledge needed, and the required personal characteristics. The best way to go about this is by asking someone who performs the job to help you determine the essential job tasks and the essential skills required. It could even be the person leaving the job or even someone doing the same job at another company.

3. Assess your candidates according to your defined criteria.

Plan ahead with a set of questions that you'll use before you begin interviewing potential candidates or checking their references. Use a planned structure with the same questions for each candidate to make the interviewing process more productive. Have someone else whose judgment you respect also interviewing the candidates for the purpose of objectivity.

4. Gather more information from your reference checks by asking previous employers and supervisors those questions that can't simply be answered "yes" or "no."

For example, ask "What advice would you give me for hiring this candidate?", rather than "Would you consider hiring this person?" Of course, this may or may not work because some companies may only be able to provide you with yes or no answers. If that's the case, then ask questions such as, "If you had the chance to hire this person again would you?"

5. Ask the interview panel if working with this person doesn't work out, what could be the most likely reason and how would it affect the company?

This will reveal your doubts and concerns. You may feel that the flaws of this candidate could be corrected with a little more training. If you feel the candidate might be difficult to supervise -- do more of an assessment before you hire.

How do you ensure they will do well in your trucking company? You can employ the following methods to determine this.

a) Find out how they react under pressure- the trucking company is a very complex work environment, things need to be done quickly, accurately, and effectively. This then means that your employees need to work well under stressful situations. You can create a culture that reduces stress, but you can never create one with no stress at all. By identifying their stressors, you can determine whether or not they will be a good fit, but also learn more about how to support them when things get hectic.

b) Give candidates the chance to weed themselves out- In your trucking company, there will only be some employees who can handle the stress. You would be surprised at the differences between candidates when it comes to their ability to perform professionally during the hiring process. The right candidate should impress you with the timing and execution of the steps you ask them to follow.

c) Empower your team to play a hand in the process- If you already have some employees, it's a good idea to involve them in the selection process. This is because they're your best option for a second opinion. They know the business and know what works best for the company. This also helps share the vision, culture, and team with the candidate. It helps them visualize the team they will be working with.

Best Ways to Encourage and Motivate Employees to Do a Good Job

As a new business owner, the most important aspects you need to focus on are maximizing profits and enhancing productivity in order to keep your business going. To achieve these, you need your team of employees to work efficiently. Motivated employees will always strive to perform better. The following are some of the ways you can motivate your employees:

1. Communicate better

It is important that you do not overlook communication. Ensure that you regularly communicate with your employees regularly and in person.

By doing so, you will make them feel valuable. One on one communication is also the best way to go when you want to express your gratitude for their great job.

Your employees should not have to learn about issues concerning the company through rumors. Thus, it is important that you update them on any changes in the company. This will maintain the team spirit.

2. Be an example

As their leader, you must portray a good example. Positivity and good moods are infectious and your employees will follow suit. You cannot expect them to be everything that you are not. Things like believing in them will, in turn, make them believe in themselves and thus they'll be more productive.

3. Empower them

Allow your employees to contribute in terms of ideas. By giving them room to share their suggestions, it helps in improving performance.

It does not end at listening to their contribution but also considering their advice and implementing it. If you only ask and then fail to make use of their suggestions, they will stop sharing their views.

Ensure that you give them the authority to make decisions as long as they are not negative and are in line with the company's policy.

4. Offer advancement opportunities

Knowing that they are working towards something better or greater keeps your employees more motivated. They will have much to work for if they believe there is an opportunity for advancement.

Nobody wants to remain stuck in their career. Offering your employees training will motivate them by acquiring skills that will help them move up in their career.

By equipping them for better opportunities, your company

earns a good reputation as well as the title of one of the best companies to work in.

5. Provide incentives

The best way of motivating employees is through incentives. You don't have to get expensive things but rather something that helps you to express your appreciation. For instance gift cards, movie tickets, an extra day off with pay, or even rewards such as bonuses are all great examples of incentives.

Motivation should not be a once in a while kind of thing—it should be consistent. Motivation is critical in keeping the best employees, otherwise you will be facing a high turnover rate.

Running Background Tests and Drug Tests

It is vital to know the background of your potential employee. Running background checks, therefore, comes in handy. Federal and state regulations regarding these checks need to be followed. This section will show you a legal, safe and accurate way of performing a background check.

Select a background check service

Most companies seek the services of background check services for the following reasons:

a) It helps save time

b) It protects your company from a lawsuit

c) Fast and accurate results are guaranteed

A manual background check is expensive in terms of costs

and time. Long hours will be spent contacting various government databases and courthouses not forgetting that using the wrong information for the purpose of making a hiring decision exposes your company to a hefty lawsuit. For these reasons pick a background check service.

Performing a background check on your own

Though it will take you more time and it's expensive as well as legally dangerous, you could conduct a manual background check. Fees are charged for accessing various government records. Some of the records that you can legally access include:

Social networks - Use their profile information on social media to decide on the candidate.

Use a national sex offender registry database to know whether they have ever been convicted of a sexual crime.

Department of motor vehicles– this will be to obtain driving records, which can be done by mail or just by going to their office in person.

Education institutions – to verify their education certificates as indicated on the resume.

Previous employers – to establish their work ethics, experience, and general conduct.

Note that you will need permission from the potential employee to conduct a background check whether it is done via a background check service or done manually. The person must sign an authorization form which will show his consent for the background check regardless of the information you are searching for. After the candidate has signed the authorization form, you can then proceed to conduct all the searches mentioned above.

Conducting a background check is, therefore, best done by combining both the manual check and background check service which will be more accurate and detailed.

Drug-testing employees

Job applicants may be required to be screened for drug and alcohol use. According to the state law and company policy, employers may do this prior to making a job offer or as a contingency for an offer. Employees may also be tested for drugs or alcohol in the workplace, as permitted by state law.

A variety of employment-related drug and alcohol tests are used by employers. Types of drug tests showing the presence of drugs or alcohol include urine drug tests, blood drug tests, hair drug tests, breath alcohol tests, saliva drug screens, and sweat drug screens.

Types of Drug tests:

Blood Drug and Alcohol Tests

Blood drug tests may be requested when job applicants or employees are screened for illegal drugs. It involves measuring the amount of alcohol or drugs in the blood at the time of the screening. This will test for amphetamines, cocaine, marijuana, methamphetamines, opiates, and alcohol.

Breath Alcohol Tests

Breathalyzers are alcohol testing devices commonly used for measuring how much alcohol is currently in the blood. Breath alcohol tests can't show past usage. Generally, an ounce of alcohol lasts up to an hour in a person's system.

Mouth Swab Drug and Alcohol Tests

A mouth swab drug test is administered by collecting saliva from inside the person's mouth. The saliva is tested for any evidence of drugs used during the previous few hours and up to one to two days prior to the test.

Chapter 6: The Best Ways to Get Freight for Your Business

This chapter covers the various options you can use to obtain freight for your trucking company and also addresses the pros and cons of each option. It will discuss the type of freight to haul by looking at the different types of freight available, the modes of freight, and the various types of truck freight and trailers that are available in the market.

Trucking involves transportation of cargo but just like any other business, it's important to know how to get freight and ensure that your business remains active in order to make profits. The following are the options available for getting freight for your business. We will also take you through the pros and cons of each option:

Freight brokers – Freight brokers connect shippers to truckers. Freight brokers do most of the difficult work, which includes negotiation of rates with shippers. They're good to consider if you're just starting out. Freight brokers make money by facilitating a business transaction between a carrier and a shipper.

Pros

- Freight brokers help to save time, resources and money as they act as your shipping department without incurring the expense of actually having your own. At the same time, they eliminate the need for conducting training and spending time on invoices. This enables you to invest more time into your business.

- As your business goes through various cycles, a freight broker offers flexibility and scalability by providing you with a large or small freight capacity.

- Working with a freight broker will offer you a learning platform since brokers have shipping expertise.

- Freight brokers open your business to a wider network of customers in terms of shippers who have buying power which would reduce your shipping expenses. They also give you access to capacity which would either be too costly for your business or otherwise unavailable.

- Working with a freight broker creates a partnership that ensures your company's best interest since your loss is their loss and your gain is also their gain.

Cons

- Freight brokers minimize the profits of your trucking company because when they negotiate, they usually only think of making a sale. They could accept the lowest price, leaving the carrier who agrees to this cost with low-profit margins.

- Freight brokers have the power to cancel a load despite a carrier having received a confirmation since they are their own boss.

Dispatch Services - For a startup in this business you could consider hiring a dispatcher directly or get a contract with a dispatch service to help get your business up and running.

Most of them can also provide back office services such as accounting, billing, and collections. Dispatch services vary in the services they offer since there are those who offer end to end services. This would include things such as finding a load or ensuring that shippers pay invoices. Some of the services offered by dispatchers include finding loads, assigning loads, managing the drivers, maintaining motor carrier compliance, handling arising issues, providing customer service, and handling administrative activities like billing and collection.

The cost of freight dispatchers is negotiable, and it can either be based on a flat rate or a percentage of the load. The following are the pros and cons of working with a freight dispatcher:

Pros

- A freight dispatcher eases the burden of having to find loads since they can offer end to end services as discussed above.

- Freight dispatchers enable you to have a learning experience since they have the expertise in the shipping business.

- They also reduce paperwork on your end hence you can utilize that extra time you'll save to help grow your business.

Cons

- Freight dispatchers are expensive. A full dispatcher's salary ranges between $30,000 and $50,000 per year.

- Freight dispatchers also reduce the amount of profit

you would have kept since their salaries are included.

Load boards – A load board is an online system that connects shippers directly to carriers. Load boards are very convenient because there are so many listings with clear details making it easier for a carrier to decide what he or she wants according to his or her business preferences.

Some load boards are free while others charge a monthly fee and offer better options. This does not mean that the free load boards are bad.

Any opportunity you have to earn business is encouraged. Load boards are a good option for those people who are just starting their business. The following are the pros and cons of using a load board:

Pros

- Load boards are online and always accessible.
- They enable truckers to find loads that match their services.
- They offer access to credit information, giving you the power to decide who to work with based on that information.
- They provide a platform for getting feedback from customers that you have worked with.
- They eliminate the occurrence of not having a full capacity truck when transporting cargo, meaning more revenue for you.
- Some load boards are free or inexpensive.

Cons

- Some load boards will cause you to incur costs.

- It can risky since you're doing business with people you don't know that well.

- Freight brokers are involved in load board transactions, and therefore minimizing your company's revenue.

- It's highly competitive since most carriers use it to get customers for their services.

- You will mostly work for a low rate when using load boards because shippers have the upper hand and it's overcrowded with carriers.

Registering as a Government contractor – The U.S government is one of the largest shippers that frequently outsource staffing needs. Trucking falls under one of these needs and they're looking for owner-operators and small carriers like you. Both the state and local government are in need of trucking services. It requires registration and a few other steps. You can get all the information from your local or state government office.

Pros

- They offer good pay.

- It's easier to get a job with the government as a contractor than other government jobs.

- The application process is through a different website and not the one for any other U.S. government job.

- You get the benefit of work-life balance since you operate the same hours as the other employees.

Cons

- Unlike the rest of the government employees whose jobs are secure, a contractor can be fired any time.

- You won't get to enjoy the privileges enjoyed by the other government employees since they see you as an external person.

- You're not assigned a specific person to report to and you'll have multiple bosses.

Prospecting-Prospecting involves learning about the shippers within your area by conducting research. Many companies in freight businesses find contracts through prospecting. To make contact you'll need to cold call, email them, or just go knocking on their doors. You will start by introducing yourself then proceed to ask about their trucking needs. It does not end there, you will have to keep checking in with them just in case an opportunity comes up. Prospecting does not guarantee that you'll land a customer. The following are the pros and cons of prospecting:

Pros

- Prospecting eventually helps build relationships as you keep checking on your prospects.

- It gets easier with time. You'll only get better at connecting with prospective clients.

- Persistence usually wins. The shippers are usually willing to give you a chance if you're persistent.

Cons

- There is a lot of resistance when trying to convince shippers to trust your company.

- Many shippers have long-term relationships with carriers and are unwilling to make changes.

- Prospecting does not guarantee that you get the job.

Networking – Networking is the most common avenue for most business startups, trucking included to obtain new clients. It involves joining associations in the trucking industry and attending events that are also attended by shippers.

You can get fast and accessible information on what is going on in your industry through internet research. You just need to meet new people and shake hands.

By doing so, you're able to create awareness about your trucking business and you'll be someone familiar as opposed to a stranger. Networking pays off for most businesses.

It offers the opportunity for you to interact and learn from others who have been where you are right now and have grown their businesses from scratch.

The following are the pros and cons of networking:

Pros

- People tend to do business with people they know. Networking enables you to interact with people in your industry and allows you to become recognizable in the business.

- Networking helps your personal development and

allows the opportunity of gaining exposure.

- Networking helps you to step out of your comfort zone.

- By knowing more about your industry than others, you get to become the expert.

- Not only is networking good for business, but it could also be the place you make good friends.

Cons

- It's time-consuming since there are always many events. It's best to pick the most important events to you.

- It takes time to gain trust and earn business.

- Most of these events have fees that can be expensive to maintain.

- There are always personality conflicts. You can't get along with everyone.

Types of Freight

Freight is a large load (usually on pallets) that exceeds the weight or size that is handled by small parcel carriers. It's important to note that the type of freight that you carry determines where you get the freight. To give you a better understanding, we will cover the different types of freight, the modes of freight, and truck and trailer types. There are three types of freight:

1. **Less than Truckload (LTL)**

LTL contains shipments that do not fill the trailer truck completely. Today, most truck trailers are 8' – 8.5' wide, 12.5' – 13.5' high, and 40' – 53' long. Due to this size, LTL shipments can be loaded into a single truck and several customers and destinations can be serviced. LTL freight shipments usually weigh between 100 and 20,000 lbs depending on the carrier.

2. Partial Truckload (PT)

Shipments that do not fill the truck completely are known as a partial truckload. Similar to full truckload shipments, they usually remain on a single truck. They're subjected to less handling than LTL shipments. The average partial truckload shipment falls between LTL and FTL weight and sizes. The way it's transported is the main difference between LTL and FTL and not the sizes or weight.

3. Full Truckload (FTL)

All freight shipments that fully occupy a trailer are known as a full truckload. This involves heavyweight or volume shipments from point to point. Weight limits are determined by the truck's weight and local laws. In the US it's usually 34,000 to 45,000 lbs.

Modes of freight

1. Air freight

This is the transportation of freight using a cargo plane. It involves transporting goods to the airport of origin first, flying them to the destination airport then transporting the goods using trucks to the final destination. This is the costliest method of transporting goods but it's also the fastest between two destinations. Air freight is not allowed to carry hazardous materials and other prohibited goods.

2. Sea/Ocean freight

Sea or ocean freight involves transportation of goods from port to port via sea or ocean. Shipments are divided into two groups; FCL (full container load) and LCL (less than container load). The sizes of the containers are 20', 40' or 53' in length. Depending on your needs, the providers offer expedited and economy options. A limit to sea or ocean-based freight is proximity to a serviceable port, which is made possible by using trucks to and from the ports or by trains.

3. Rail freight

This is the transportation of goods over land via a railcar. Depending on the needs of the shipper, shipments are arranged from individual railcars to entire trains. A wide variety of special railcars can be used to carry individual railcar shipments such as intermodal cars, ore cars, and triple-decker car carriers. Trains can only be used to carry goods where rail tracks are available. Trucks are used to transport the goods to and from railways.

4. Intermodal freight

Intermodal freight involves a combination of any transport modes such as a truck, train, plane, and ship. To ensure the most economical and timely outcome, intermodal enables shipments to maximize the benefits of each mode. Intermodal can take a single origin shipment and deliver the same shipment to several destinations. Limitations of intermodal freight involve multiple handling situations, which can lead to damages as well as specific organization requirements of each mode.

Truck freight and Trailer types

- **Dry van freight–** These are trailers that are covered with a flat deck. Van trailers are the most common trailers used for transporting freight. They have a box body that offers cover to the load to protect it from weather elements as well as security to the load.

- **Refrigerated (Reefer) freight-** Refrigerated freights are shipments that require a trailer with a regulated temperature. Refrigerated trailers come with a large capacity climate control unit fitted on the front of the trailer that operates on an extra fuel supply. The trailer can be partitioned to provide temperature control to a particular section. Generally, refrigerated shipments consist of perishable food, chemicals or medical supplies.

- **Oversized freight-** Any load exceeding the standard legal size and/or weight limits for a certain route is considered an oversized freight. In most of the US, these are loads that are wider than 8' 6" or taller than 13' 6". Also belonging to the oversized group are excessively long loads (combination length) or heavy (total or per axle). These regulations may vary from state to state. There are also limitations on the roads and bridges that must be taken into consideration. Careful planning of particular routes is key. Additionally, the truck is accompanied by one or several pilot cars that warn motorists of the oncoming truck to ensure route safety and control the transportation as a safety measure.

- **Flatbed freight-** Any load that is put on a flatbed trailer is known as flatbed freight. Flatbed loads are exposed to weather elements and need to be secured by the driver. Due to their open nature, flatbeds allow certain loads to be loaded with safety and greater speed since it's possible to use a crane rather than a forklift. It allows loading to be done from either side and can accommodate loads of full width. Flatbeds are very common and widely used for transporting industrial loads or construction materials.

- **Lowboy freight-** Being very similar to flatbed loads, Lowboy trailers are designed with a much lower deck height, which functionally lowers the total height of the load in order to prevent it from falling into the category of oversized load restrictions. This enables transportation of taller loads without the extra costs and safety issues of an oversized load.

Chapter 7: Common Mistakes that Could Run You Out of Business

So far, our focus has been all about what you should do and the steps you should take when starting your trucking business. There have been many scenarios where people have overlooked mistakes, which are mostly avoidable but end up costing them their business.

Therefore, this chapter will cover some of the mistakes that you should avoid based on the experience of those who have been down that road before you. It will also familiarize you with some of the situations you can expect to encounter within the very first year in the trucking business.

You'll gain the insight that you need to run a trucking business. The main aim is to leave no room for surprises. Brace yourself as I take you through what will soon be your reality.

As we stated earlier, one of the things that will help you navigate your trucking business to success is constantly learning more about the trucking industry since everything is subject to change. Learning, as you know does not only entail the positive attributes but also the negative.

It's good to learn about the negatives before you indulge in the business and find yourself making the same mistakes. We'll go over some of the most common mistakes that beginners in the trucking business make.

The mistakes are so numerous that I can't exhaust them all

here. The following should be of help to you as you start your journey in this industry. They include:

1. **Growing too fast**

As much as you want to see your business grow, it is important to ensure that you do not do it too fast lest you cause harm. For example, over-booking loads and missing ETA's because you didn't plan accordingly could negatively affect your reputation. Starting to employ people unnecessarily could lower your revenue since salaries are one of the most expensive costs of your operation.

2. **Not meeting the new entrant guidelines**

According to the new entrant guidelines, all new fleets that have registered with the department of transportation (DOT) are subject to an audit within the first 18 months of being in business. The wrong assumption by new entrants is that they have until 18 months to meet all the stated guidelines before they can be audited. Well, that is not the case because there are new entrants that have had to go through auditing on the 3rd month of operation and had to be shut down for 30 days to allow them to meet the requirements. Such shutdowns could run your business into bankruptcy.

The following are the violations of the CSA safety audit that new entrants normally fail:

Alcohol and Drug Violations

- No alcohol and/or drug testing programs.
- No random alcohol and/or drug testing programs.
- Using a driver who refused to take a required alcohol or drug test.

- Using a driver the company knows had a blood alcohol content of 0.04 or greater.

- Using a driver who failed to complete required follow-up procedures after testing positive for drugs.

Driver Violations

- Using a driver without a valid CDL.

- Using a disqualified driver.

- Using a driver with a revoked, suspended, or canceled CDL.

- Using a medically unqualified driver.

Operation Violations

- Operating a motor vehicle without having the required level of insurance.

- Failing to require drivers to make hours-of-service records.

Repair and Inspection Violations

- Operating a vehicle declared out-of-service for safety deficiencies before repairs are made.

- Not performing OOS repairs reported in driver-vehicle inspection reports (DVIRs).

- Operating a CMV not periodically inspected.

3. Not having enough insurance coverage

Most new entrants meet the basic guidelines of having liability and cargo insurance coverage. It's vital that you also get physical damage of non-owned trailer coverage as well as general liability coverage, which protects your driver and others in case the truck is not involved.

Note that depending on your fleet size and type, workers compensation coverage may be needed as well. Make sure you understand all of your business needs and get the correct coverage based on that. A lack of proper insurance coverage has led to some trucking businesses being incapable of paying for damages.

4. Not understanding your true cost per mile

As discussed earlier you must understand both your businesses' fixed costs and variable costs. Just as a reminder, fixed costs are expenses automatically incurred whether your truck is running or parked.

An example of fixed costs would include things like insurance and rent. Variable costs are the unpredictable costs such as truck maintenance and fuel costs.

When you're starting your business you should have enough cash to cover your business expenses for 3 to 6 months since you'll need to cover these costs before your business starts earning any money. Keep in mind that in the beginning, it's not a guarantee that your business will grow as fast as you expect. In order to manage your cash flow, it's important that you know the right cost per mile.

Your other business financial reports and the cost per mile are a measure of your business' financial health. You should be able to understand your basic cost per mile based on the annual expenses of your trucks and their annual mileage.

This can be achieved by dividing the annual costs by the number of miles covered that year. The challenge, however, is allocating all the expenses accurately. This is the main reason most businesses don't survive. Most new trucking businesses fail to take the time to understand their cost per mile, their expenses, and how to document these expenses. In addition, they accept almost any rate offered just to get a load. Before they know it, they encounter problems with their cash flow. This means that they become unable to pay their bills, drivers are not making them enough money, and eventually the business starts crumbling.

5. Being cheap about marketing

Most new trucking businesses do not understand the magnitude of promoting and marketing their business. Most new ventures think that word of mouth and a few fliers will do, but this isn't always the case.

Your marketing strategy will determine whether your business sinks or floats. Marketing, just like other factors involved requires strategic planning.

Start by identifying the area that you want your business to cover and research prospective customers. Then decide on the media you'll employ, which includes opening a page on social media and being active.

This will help to create awareness. You can also create memorable and relevant business cards, make posters, get ad space in your local business magazine or newspaper, etc. Marketing is the backbone of every business and it's where you'll get most of your leads.

Ensure that you allocate enough resources for marketing. In the beginning, it will be costlier but once your business gains ground, you will have established your brand and ultimately realize that marketing pays off.

6. Hiring the wrong employees

Hiring employees is not an easy task and it should involve a thorough process as discussed earlier. This is possible by first identifying what it is that your business needs. This is also in line with whether you need employees. As we pointed out earlier, hiring unnecessarily will just increase your costs of salary and eat into your revenue. You should consider outsourcing certain tasks when needed as a cheaper alternative.

7. Lack of a clear written plan

It's paramount that you have a clear plan for your business and it should be written. The goals should be achievable and relevant. Aim to also have an inspiring vision for your business because your mission will make it possible to achieve your vision in the future. Lacking a good plan has led to most startups getting stuck along the way. Some to the extent of shutting down because they did not put much thought into their business plan.

8. Listening to family and friends

I know this sounds weird because these are the people you trust the most. However, they may be lacking the experience needed to run a trucking business, yet they want to give you advice on the topic. Take their advice with a grain of salt if they don't have any experience in the industry. You wouldn't take financial advice from someone who's broke and the same premise applies here.

9. Unexpected expenses

Most new owner-operators are under the assumption that just because they purchased a brand-new truck, there will be no need for maintenance costs or costs incurred as a result of the truck breaking down. They end up eliminating this cost while budgeting hence affecting their business revenue.

10. **Assuming there will always be work**

Most new trucking business ventures live under the illusion that once they start the company, they will always be busy. The reality is that it will take time to build up a client list and it requires a lot of patience and persistence to get your business to a high-income level.

What should you expect in your first year of starting your trucking business?

As a beginner in the trucking business, you may have wondered how the first year will be. Truth be told, everyone in the trucking business has a different experience. Nevertheless, there are those experiences that are unanimous to everyone and those are the ones we are going to look at. They include:

1. **Living on a budget**

You must employ money management skills that will help get you through the first year in the trucking business. I'm sure you have ambitious goals, but make sure that they are realistic. Base your budget on yearlong averages as opposed to what you are earning from the business currently. Estimate that owner-operators make an average of around $140,000 annually. Understand that until your business becomes established, expect to be on the lower end of what owner-operators make. There are several other factors that will affect your first-year earnings. These factors include insurance fees, truck maintenance expenses, fuel, inspections, equipment required for tracking hours, software, and slow seasons when cash flow is low.

2. Less than desirable loads

Before you can be picky about the loads that you haul, in the first year expect to carry just about anything that you can find. You must start somewhere.

Be prepared to make trips and have loads involving route deviations, weekends, holidays, or even evening hours. The upside of this is that by maintaining schedules and making contacts in this first year, your good reputation grows, and you'll eventually find yourself dealing with better loads and landing long-term contracts that are mutually beneficial.

3. Less home time

Work-home balance is the first adjustment you'll have to make as an owner-operator when you start your trucking business. As you try to establish your trucking business, you might not get to spend as much time at home as you'd like to. Going by the 70-hour maximum hour restriction over eight days, an average trucker is always traveling between 2,000 to 3,000 hours every week. However, as you become established, you'll be able to create schedules that meet your wishes. This will help balance your time better.

4. Getting driving experience

In the first year, you'll still be learning how to be a good truck driver as an owner-operator. In the event that you have to hire a driver or two, they must have good driving experience. More experience means making more money since better driving will ensure timely delivery. You'll also be able to relax while driving.

Ultimately, getting to talk to a seasoned owner-operator who has gone through the ups and downs will give you a better understanding of what to expect during your first year in the business.

Chapter 8: The Proper Trucking Business Mindset You Must Have in Order to Succeed

This chapter will give insight into the importance of your mindset in business. It will shed light on how to control your reactions through the business seasons or when things do not work out as planned.

Mindset is someone's general attitude and mental state and how they react in various situations.

Everyone in business desires to be successful. Many times, people question why some people are successful, and why others are not? The fact is that your mindset seriously determines your level of success.

If you want to be successful in business, you must have the right attitude, flexibility, and passion for what you do. Success has no room for any kind of negativity.

The only difference among entrepreneurs is the way in which they perceive things. We hold different perceptions about things and that's what makes everyone unique. Perception is the reason why there are successful entrepreneurs and not so successful entrepreneurs.

The following is a list of the attitudes that you need to adopt if you want to succeed in your business. They are:

Be courageous

You can't afford to be afraid if you become an entrepreneur. You'll never be the successful entrepreneur that you aspire to be if you're afraid. Being successful means doing more than just the ordinary. The only way you'll learn and eventually better yourself is by never being afraid to fail.

Set goals

For you to be successful you must set realistic goals and work on timelines. Setting goals will help to ensure that you work hard towards achieving them. Ensure that the goals you set are clearly defined. You also want to make sure that you actually write down your goals instead of just keeping them in your head. When you write your goals down, it makes them real as opposed to just an idea in your head.

Choose your company wisely

The saying that birds of the same feather flock together also applies in the business world. Surround yourself with people who can add value to your vision or people who share the same vision as you.

It's very easy to spread negativity, in fact, it's said that negativity is infectious. Avoid all the negative people in your life and you'll see a big difference.

Be selective

It's vital that you always see the bigger picture. See things for more than what they really are. By doing so, you'll know what is expected and needed in order to succeed. Always be mindful and aware of everything that is happening around you. Know your competitors, who you can collaborate with for mutual benefit, market needs, etc. This will help you to prevent making mistakes in the future.

When the time comes that you need to choose your team, being selective will also play a major role. Ensure that you know everyone you work with in terms of their strengths and weaknesses. This will help you in placing them in the right departments. Being selective will eventually lead you to success.

Take risks

Success involves taking risks most of the time. There is never a guarantee that what you're doing will lead you to success. It's all a matter of trying and seeing what works. Taking risks is a great challenge, but without taking risks you will never rise to the level you want. Like they say, you never know until you try.

Listen to your instincts

We all have instincts and it's important to have confidence in your instincts. Other than basing your business decisions on research and available data, listen to your inner self. A winning mindset requires that you sometimes make decisions with your gut feeling. In the long run, you'll realize that it's all worth it.

Avoid stagnation

If you ever feel like there is no more to learn in your professional or personal life, realize that it's time to make changes. It's time to leave your comfort zone. In order to grow, you should always avoid stagnation. By stepping out of your comfort zone, you'll encounter new challenges and overcome new obstacles.

Think of failure as a learning opportunity

Failure creates the best learning opportunity. Staying the

same year after year but not necessarily failing means that you are not challenging yourself enough.

It's important to develop a mindset that views failure as a learning experience. By so doing, you will have reframed failure and taking risks will then become easier. This mindset will also make you less prone to anxiety which is vital for a winning attitude.

Developing a successful mindset takes time. It's important to put all of the above factors into consideration and apply them to your business. Remember that nothing in business is easy, in fact, it will be one of the toughest journeys in your life but a positive mindset will always make it better. Overcoming adversity will help you to develop faith in yourself.

How to Look at Money Spent as an Investment

Starting a business can be very costly, as it requires you to invest both your time and money.

Most new entrepreneurs try to hoard their savings and spend as little as possible on their business. Yes, you should have some money saved in case of an emergency, but being too conservative with your money won't help you grow at a good pace.

Don't be afraid to invest money into your business. Often times people are afraid to invest money into something that isn't making money yet, but that could be the very reason why the business isn't making any money.

Also, the number of essential costs can really weigh down a business owner. As business owners make plans during the early stages of operation, they will check off some of the essential requirements as not necessary or too expensive and might postpone them for later when they become more established.

Spending money on these essential things will determine your long-term productivity and will set you apart from your competitors in the long run. Therefore, some expenses are worth the sacrifice and will eventually be worth it in the near future.

Spending money on the following is an investment:

Equipment

Having the right tools in your business is critical. When it comes to execution of your trucking business speed and efficiency really matter. Ensure that you have the right mobile devices, a working computer, and of course a truck.

Buying the latest and greatest equipment is not necessary. Every purchase is an investment in the future of the business.

The right workspace

Make sure that you have a comfortable and inviting workspace or office. This doesn't mean that it has to be lavish; rather it just needs to be a place that excites you and others to work in. As long as you don't make the mistake of spending money to create a workspace for the purpose of impressing other people you'll be good to go.

The right team

As your business grows, you'll eventually find yourself overwhelmed and will seek help by hiring employees. At first, you may hire on a part-time basis. Don't wait too long to get the help you need for fear of incurring costs. The truth is, not hiring people at the right time will slow down the growth of your company.

When you find there are things to be done that need the skills and experience you're lacking, it's only right that you invest in employees. The right team of employees will be your greatest investment, so make sure that you take the time necessary to hire the right people.

Market research

While making your business plan, don't hesitate to invest in conducting market research. You don't want to make the mistake of assuming what it is that other people want. By actually going out and talking to your prospective customers whether online or in person, you'll be able to figure out exactly what their pain points are that they need to be solved.

Branding

Building your brand early sets your business up for success. Since you only get to brand your company once, it's vital to get it right. Branding will connect you with your customers by making your service the preferred choice. Strong branding is also linked to business performance that drives consumer behavior. If your product or service is relevant and unique, customers will be drawn in, which means more revenue for your business.

Social media management

Many new business owners see social media as unnecessary because they don't know how to use it or because they consider it a waste of time. Spending money on social media platforms helps in keeping your customers engaged as you'll have active followers who will be interested in what you have to say, and in turn, it will help spread your message.

Having an audience helps build authority by sharing your knowledge with them on social media. With time you'll become an expert in your business and eventually, more customers will seek your services. Whatever platforms you use, it's a great investment for your business, so be sure to not skip out on it.

Company culture

Company culture is your company's personality based on the people inside your work environment. Everything from how you work to their benefits constitutes the company culture. Building a company culture is very vital as you start up since it helps build your company's foundation. Having loyal and engaged employees is very valuable to your business. Offer bonuses and incentives when possible. Also, recognize their effort by offering gifts, and you'll soon have motivated employees who will be more productive.

Education and training

You should aim to spend money on educating and training your employees. This is a good investment because they will apply their new knowledge in their work and produce a better output.

Software

Spending money on software solutions is a good investment because as discussed earlier, they enhance efficiency and quality of service.

How to Stay Calm

It's important to stay calm and not let business challenges give you anxiety. The reality is that in business, just like in real life, there are ups and downs. Regardless of the situation, you should always strive to keep going and give it your best shot.

The following are some of the ways that can help you stay calm when you're about to make an important decision:

a) Taking a deep breath

By taking deep breaths, you allow oxygen to circulate in your brain, resulting in relaxation. With your brain fully functional, you'll be in a position to make better decisions or still realize the options that are available. Taking lots of deep breaths will help you to physically and mentally stay calm.

b) Focus on the outcome

The worst thing you can do is to react negatively in an emergency situation. Unfortunately, this is what people often do and it can have a lasting impact on your business. Small bumps in the road are also bound to happen but don't let them derail you from your goals. Take a moment to focus on the outcome or the bigger picture. This will allow you to make decisions based on perspective. This, in turn, will help you navigate toward the desired final outcome.

c) Work out

Physical exercise helps reduce anxiety, stress and even anger. All of these conditions are common during difficult times in business. Working out and staying physically active will help you stay calm.

If you need to make a decision or you're about to make an important call, try taking a walk or going for a run before you act. This is especially important before making any big decisions since it enables you to keep calm.

d) Listen to others

Staying calm can sometimes mean being silent while allowing others to express their views. When you open up to listening, it allows you to stay calm. Listening is a cultured skill that can neutralize many difficult situations.

e) Empathize

Empathizing involves you looking at a situation from the viewpoint of another person. Listening and empathizing helps to bring your mind to a calm solution or suggestion that could prove to be useful. Learning to empathize will ensure that you do not take things personally. Attacks that might have set you off in the past will now become opportunities and you'll begin to see that what people say about you is actually something that they themselves are struggling with.

f) Stick to your guns

Being able to listen and empathize does not mean that you have to change your decisions. Once your mind is made up, you can be calm in whatever challenge you are facing by sticking to your guns about the decision. Being unwavering will help you to remain calm as well.

g) Know your value

Just like being firm in your decisions, knowing your value, will enable you not to take things personally and you will be able to keep calm. When life gets tough in some way or when someone tries to worsen the situation, knowing your value will help you to remain calm and perform according to your own expectations. It will also help you to earn respect from others. Always remember that there is only one of you. Treat obstacles as temporary setbacks and you'll, therefore, be able to bounce back more quickly.

h) Be Forgiving

Entrepreneurs know that losing your cool will happen from time to time. That is why you need to be quick to forgive. Avoid holding any grudges. Being quick to forgive will help you to maintain your inner peace that allows you to remain calm in the face of adversity.

i) Focus on the good

Focusing on the good will help you see all of life's opportunities. When you see challenges as the stimulant for new opportunities, you'll be able to stay calm during the trials of life.

j) Be clear on your evaluation criteria

Basing your evaluation on your values and goals will determine what is important to you. You should apply a scoring system, which will evaluate each task, activity, or opportunity. While the scores are important, the process will tell you more because you will discover what is important and what is not. Therefore, you'll be able to make decisions according to your own standards.

k) Set a timeline and a deadline

It's important to create a timeline and deadline for the sole purpose of knowing when to make certain decisions. When there is time allocated for research and exploration, it allows you to have all the relevant information at hand, enabling you to make the best choice. This also offers a foundation for making the decision based on a vast knowledge of the project. Working on a deadline eliminates decision making anxiety.

l) Stay on mission

Referring to the business mission is a great tool. Asking yourself if the action you are about to take will move you closer to achieving your company's mission will help you make better decisions. If the answer is no, don't spend more time on that task trying to figure it out. If the answer is yes and the necessary resources needed are available, then go ahead and execute.

m) Clarify the consequences

The anxiety of making decisions comes from the fear of making a mistake and having to suffer the consequences. The more importance you place on a decision, the more difficult and anxious you become. Realize that there are no wrong decisions apart from the consequences that they bring with them. Making a list of the consequences according to making or not making a decision will clarify the choice you need to make.

Conclusion

The trucking industry is still a promising industry with a lot of opportunities for those who are interested in getting started. Just like starting any other business, it will require that you have patience, perseverance, and an urge to learn.

You're now familiar with everything from where to start, how to start, what trucking entails, what to expect, and everything in between.

By following the guidelines in this book, you'll greatly increase your chances of success.

www.ingramcontent.com/pod-product-compliance
Lightning Source LLC
Chambersburg PA
CBHW030650220526
45463CB00005B/1711